PENGUIN

WITH

Suzanne Finnamore is the author of the bestselling novel *Otherwise Engaged* and *The Zygote Chronicles*, which was the *Washington Post* Book of the Year in 2002. She is a journalist and has written for *Marie Claire* and *Glamour*, amongst many others. She lives in northern California with her son.

Suzanne Finnamore

SPLIT

A Story of Love,
Betrayal and Divorce

PENGUIN BOOKS

PENGUIN BOOKS

Published by the Penguin Group
Penguin Books Ltd, 80 Strand, London WC2R 0RL, England
Penguin Group (USA) Inc., 375 Hudson Street, New York, New York 10014, USA
Penguin Group (Canada), 90 Eglinton Avenue East, Suite 700, Toronto, Ontario, Canada M4P 2Y3
(a division of Pearson Penguin Canada Inc.)
Penguin Ireland, 25 St Stephen's Green, Dublin 2, Ireland
(a division of Penguin Books Ltd)
Penguin Group (Australia), 250 Camberwell Road,
Camberwell, Victoria 3124, Australia (a division of Pearson Australia Group Pty Ltd)
Penguin Books India Pvt Ltd, 11 Community Centre,
Panchsheel Park, New Delhi – 110 017, India
Penguin Group (NZ), 67 Apollo Drive, Rosedale, North Shore 0632, New Zealand
(a division of Pearson New Zealand Ltd)
Penguin Books (South Africa) (Pty) Ltd, 24 Sturdee Avenue, Rosebank, Johannesburg 2196,
South Africa

Penguin Books Ltd, Registered Offices: 80 Strand, London WC2R 0RL, England

www.penguin.com

First published in the United States of America by Dutton,
a member of the Penguin Group (USA) Inc. 2008
First published in Great Britain by Penguin Books 2009
1

Grateful acknowledgement for permission to reprint is made to: *Lives and Loves of
a She Devil* by Fay Weldon. Copyright © Trafalgar Square, 1995. Used with permission.

Parts of this work first appeared in the United States of America
in different forms in *O* magazine and on *Salon*.

Printed in England by Clays Ltd, St Ives plc

ISBN: 978-0-141-03212-2

www.greenpenguin.co.uk

Penguin Books is committed to a sustainable future
for our business, our readers and our planet.
The book in your hands is made from paper
certified by the Forest Stewardship Council.

For all the wives and mothers left behind

Contents

Author's Note

These pages embark on a gritty and absurd journey. My telling of divorce is probably not for the squeamish or the morally impeccable. If you are any of these things, put this book back on the shelf. Do it right now.

I've changed plenty of details and events too squalid and banal to inflict upon both you and the innocent.

It should be noted that my son and I are well and happy . . . he and his father are quite close. So there is hope, even though there is also despair and the destruction of hope. I consider divorce the most ugly word in the English language and it set me free.

SPLIT

I
Denial

We do not see things as they are.
We see things as we are.

—Anaïs Nin

Flight

By the time N left, running out of the house one evening with nothing but the clothes on his back and a voluminous gym bag, I had loved him for seven years. The die was cast.

I see it now as if it is freshly happening, the two of us facing off on a stage set, each in our appointed place for a major scene. It was a cold Friday night, the end of the week, a time primordially loaded for endings and therefore immaculate, befitting. My husband was methodical about everything he chose to do. He also had the trick of making set plans seem spontaneous.

I am wearing a fitted white shirt rolled at the sleeves, black cigarette pants, and red lipstick. I'm also wearing shoes with spike heels, something I normally don't do around the house. I want height. I am aware that I've been waiting for him, have recently started to prepare for his homecoming as I would prepare for a first date.

In our builder's grade kitchen, I am alone yet still conscious of posture and makeup, makeup I now wear every day, a dubious bow to vanity. Putting on my Face, my mother, Bunny, calls it. *War paint* is what I thought as I applied sheer foundation and eye pencil, brushing my eyebrows upward in small, intense strokes. My hands shake and I don't know why. The walls shimmer, too white; my fault: I've never been good at discerning shades of color. Makeup seems to complicate this problem, engage it. I stay with neutral tones. I check my lipstick in the chrome toaster. I am distorted, but the lines are all there.

Precisely at 6:10, he walks through the rain-spattered oak door and kisses my cheek. I breathe the scent of his neck and something else, some nascent excitement or fear. As he kisses my cheek, his sinewy hands are already on the martini shaker, mixing himself a drink. I take two chilled glasses out of the freezer, placing them next to a bucket of crushed ice. I spear olives (three) onto red plastic toothpicks; drop them into the clear icy liquid just as he is pouring out his first cocktail. He tells me I look beautiful and walks swiftly downstairs to our bedroom to change his shirt, though we have no plans that I am aware of.

I have been greeted and kissed in the smooth normalized way of a television show housewife. I am now waiting for some form of recognition that I exist beyond the second dimension, that we both exist together. The fact that it has come to this is not outside my consciousness, but it seems to be muffled. I love N and he loves me, although not as much as I love him; I accept this. We have A, our toddler son, and I am playing it through.

And yet here he comes, here it comes.

He capers up the carpeted stairs; slung over his arm is a charcoal wool blazer, his best. It is then I feel the fear itself, a small, ghastly tapping at my right shoulder.

I hand him an oversize frosted martini glass, his second in

ten, maybe five, minutes. He takes it with one hand, the other busily buttoning his fresh dress shirt, tearing out the paper collar stay, and letting its ragged length fall with uncharacteristic carelessness to the floor.

In my mind this is the formal beginning of the end: his visibly urgent need for fresh attire, the copious vodka, his odd pheromones, the unauthorized appearance of the blazer. Yet I know that this is not the real beginning of the end, this is illusion, a false start. It is only my primitive marking in time. The real genesis is forbidden to me, vis-à-vis N's inability to confess even the mildest transgressions. His beginning of all this, both psychologically and physically, has been sliced with great precision from my wifely vista. Theoretically, he wants his way without inflicting pain or suffering, this I know.

Yet he is saying something, my husband, actually several things at once, each more shocking and flamboyantly absurd than the last, like watching dozens of clowns exit a Volkswagen.

"We're different people. . . ."

I stand with a jar of garlic-stuffed olives in hand, motionless, waiting for exactly how, in his estimation, different we were, and why he is speaking to me as if someone else, a third party, were listening. Outside the kitchen window, redwoods loom silent and apart. A master shot would establish a simple wood-shingle house perched atop Madrone Canyon in the town of Larkspur, population 12,014. A split-level hodgepodge of bright rooms and jutting decks, a vase of calla lilies splayed like a white hand at the kitchen windowsill. Through three large bay windows we see a robust male and a statuesque wife and mother meeting companionably at the end of the day in Marin County, home of an elite group of perpetually concerned wealthy Californians who materialize en masse at the Sausalito Art Festival each Labor Day, purchasing signed lithographs, Zen fountains, and wind chimes. Our house is modest by county standards; it is small but well appointed with a two-car garage. There are no illegal rental units, no recreational vehicles, and no aluminum siding or driveway mechanics. Everything is up to Code, although our refrigerator is leaking. I can see a small pool of ice water at its base. I have to stop myself from cleaning it up as he stands there.

"I DESERVE HAPPINESS," N said, raising his voice.

Escalation. Oh, dear. N orates with a large, clear martini glass passing through my airspace, vodka sloshing onto the carpet in a gesture of freedom. Yet I was lulled by his predictability—once again, without preamble or rational discussion, he was stating his inalienable human right to have happiness in his life. By now this was a popular theme in our home, N's Happiness, a kind of precious yet difficult pet. It had become repertoire and had lost some of its original force. Although I'd never said so, it all sounded as whimsical as a lost pinwheel. He (we) have everything . . . gainful employment, a home, health, a sound child. Food, warmth. It ought to be enough; he shouldn't force us all to go delving on some quixotic hunt.

It's his happiness, I thought, slightly hysterical by now. Therefore he should find it on his own. Had he looked everywhere? I almost laughed; a small titter escaped my lips. From this brittle emotion I stepped off, as if from an unseen curb, into a different life.

I hear N say Divorce; and then the word Lawyer coming at me, a javelin.

I put down the olives and place my hands in my hair, tugging at its roots to create a counter sensation. I am not crying yet, but my throat burns. Updike claims if you talk about divorce it will happen. Yet we were not talking about it; I was being informed, and he was leaving at once. Intellectually, I knew this was often how it was done: quickly, like a careful exchange of hearts, a swift transplant. A heart can stop beating for a while, one can still live.

Realizing he has the stage, N warms to his topic. The term *visitation* is brandished. He is talking about visiting our son, A, as though he were a wonderful exhibit. A custodial schedule can be arranged, child support payments made. I realize with a wave of nausea that this is what his Happiness has meant: a euphemism for my removal. Hearing his tone, I know there is no possible chance of rebuttal or rescheduling; he is on a live feed to his new life.

"No matter what, you can't stop me from seeing A," he suddenly flashes.

Yet here he was, preparing to leave A. It made no sense. I am going insane. Yes. That is what's happening. Good. Insane.

"I never would. You're his *father*," I say, as if explaining a minor detail he has forgotten. My eyes are two X's in a white oval; my face, I feel certain, a vulgar cartoon. Because this isn't happening, it's some sort of exceptionally realistic holograph. A hallucination, perhaps caused by the antidepressants he urged on me last winter, or biochemical warfare.

Aghast to hear the words that involuntarily passed my lips, I stammered out the requisite clichés:

Why?

How can you do this?

What about the baby?

Why can't we talk about it?

Where will you go?

His reaction was a perfect zero. He had successfully flatlined, a technique he'd mastered by age forty. I had started talking Swahili, and N did not speak Swahili. He was sorry, but not regretful. Why should he know Swahili?

When someone says he wants a divorce, there is an inevitable exclamation point affixed to that statement, as in the statement Help! Or Fire! Therefore, there will be no thoughtful or complete answering of questions, because an exclamation point has rendered all questions moot. Fire!

In a move best described as cinematic, I slide slowly to the floor, to the white entryway tiles of our home. Like Alice, I feel suddenly small, surprised to have gone through the looking glass. Our house, I think. We knew it was ours before we'd even seen it; the very street hummed our names, two weeks back from our honeymoon in France, eight days wherein he fed me bouillabaisse from Michael's in Nice and we made love every night, often without waiting to get our clothes off. As my mind performs this nostalgic synapse, it simultaneously grasps for some way to make N stay within the door.

"You've seen a lawyer?" I finally ask, admittedly slow on the uptake, from my position on the floor.

I spy a tiny plastic Tyrannosaurus rex wreathed in dust behind the umbrella stand. *Our son,* I think. It seemed to me that I was having some sort of stroke, a kind where one's senses are alive and crackling but articulation impossible, no words to get the needed relief.

N brushes my question aside; he stares at a point on the ceiling and says, "I. Want. A. Divorce."

He is playing to the rear seats, firmly repeating words he'd said earlier, four words I was already busily trying to erase, unhear. Irrationally, I think, Will You Marry Me? Four words. I Want a Divorce. Four words. I would like time to count the letters as well, but there is no time. I can see by his face that there is no time.

I stare at his crooked and beautiful Basque features, oddly bright and alive with a defiant pleasure. His silver hair shines with some newly purchased styling product that comes in a hard stick. There is nothing soft in his usually supine body; it is drawn taut. Also there is an echo, the word *lawyer* bouncing about in my head, and *divorce,* the brute ugliness of the words covering me in a brackish film.

His mouth is a thick line that rebuffs conversation or obstacles. He puts on the blazer, shoots his cuffs. I sink a bit further because I know that this gesture, not the upcoming words, is the sign that professionals have been called in to help N achieve what is now his immediate goal. I know at once that were I to look, there would be a business card from a law firm in his wallet. And not just any law firm; he has come to a time in his life where he will trust only the services of crisp, seasoned professionals: dry cleaners that deliver, hotels with concierges, and local butchers who will preorder certified organic free-range turkeys for Thanksgiving.

I blink. Pull a deep breath in and out of my lungs; somehow I am not getting enough oxygen.

He says: "I have a lawyer. Someone in Kentfield."

Oh, dear. Kentfield: the rich white epicenter of the entire chocolate box county. The very word seemed to exude money and nefarious intent. Kentfield already in motion. I ingest this fact; I clamp my hands onto my thighs. The pace was brisk; I had to focus to keep up with all the new information. I could not look away from the slightly bulging veins in his neck and his cocked head, pointed at me with firm intent. N isn't just a vice president at a major marketing firm; he is a very skilled technical writer, used to having things his way and knowing the precise terms for everything. He knows what's coming out and what's going out. We had one of the first rear-projection televisions. It was N who taught me that technology was sexy. He had been described in conversations more than once as The King of New Media.

I was summarily presented with another factoid: a second bullet, what the police call a *double tap*. It is meant to ensure that the assailant is firmly down.

"You should get the papers next month."

Even now, after much reflection and puzzling aloud in the dark, I honestly can't say why that very evening, accepting the martini with three olives, he told me I looked beautiful; doubtless it was part of his sudden overall madness. He said it with a small smile, and I said *thank you*. Afterward came the wardrobe change, and a few minutes later he said the rest and walked out, looking natty.

"Good-bye, darling," he said.

And then drove away, his automatic window sliding up. The axis of my world snapped, sending me into a place that was black and where there was no time.

On the entryway floor I repeatedly recited the Lord's Prayer, and realized with a sucking sense of preposterous misfortune that no, I was mistaken; life was going to go right on. Minutes were passing with a terrible lethargy; the parsing of time would be harsh.

In the living room the grandmother clock struck the half hour. A was asleep beneath these floorboards. Our son was asleep and his father had left us, with me having a ministroke on the floor. This seemed, above and beyond the proposed divorce, a terrible social breach.

Yes. I regret to admit that either N is barking mad or else he is to be regarded as deliberately evil, a grotesque chimera made manifest in khaki pants. I am not ready to think of him as either insane or evil, to consider in full how I could love and have a child with such a person. I am not ready to think about anything, except ways in which this may still be averted. In my mind I reverse time as one does after a car accident, I retrace each step but end up at the same conclusion, the same large deductible. Everything happens just the same.

I make one telephone call that night, to my mother, Bunny.

"It's me. He's left."

I was still on the floor, having pulled my cell phone from the pocket of my jeans jacket, conveniently located next to the umbrella stand. There is a long pause, during which I am not crying but have the hiccups. My mother is a firm believer in the long pause, useful in interrogations, proclamations of truth, and the occasional cutting dead of someone without their knowing it.

"That son of a bitch," Bunny says.

I make no response. I listen to the heat shut off, a cessation of noise from the vent on the floorboard. Sixty-eight degrees, I think. Always.

Bunny was rapidly summing up the situation, as would Christiane Amanpour in a disheveled kibbutz, somehow managing to make sense of it all.

"He has no idea what he's done," Bunny announces.

"He seems to have his heart set on it," I mumble.

I want Bunny to contradict me, to say it's ridiculous, he's only bluffing. My mother does not do this. Bunny has been divorced once, from my late father, Richard. It happened in 1967, a vintage year for divorce. Bunny married Ron in 1969; I consider Ron my real father.

"So he's got a lawyer," Bunny said; it was not a question.

"Oh, yeah," I said, but it turned out I had shouted it. A did not wake up. We both waited on the telephone, to see if he would.

"Is A asleep, Suzanne?" Bunny asked.

"Oh, yeah," I said, softly this time, remembering that I was a mother, a terrible mistake at this point. Someone who can make things happen must be alerted.

My mother suggested they drive in from Hayward, a fortymile distance. I told her no. Bunny said she would come in the morning and to call her at any time during the night, and that A and I would be fine; she said it as though it were a threat. I half expected her to hang up and deploy a makeshift posse, but Bunny had no idea where he was, any more than I did. N could be anywhere. It was past dark, and I did not know where my husband was. Fortunately I could not dwell on this, as I had to survive the night.

Then Bunny stopped speaking. I heard my stepfather, Ron, shuffling about in the background, grabbing car keys, or maybe he was putting them away, back on their places on the wall of their town house. A B for Bunny's keys, an R for Ron's keys, both the letters shaped like hooks. My mind was doing some strange review of everything I knew to be true. I looked around our living room, everything still there. Unbelievable.

I told my mother I would see her tomorrow.

"Good," Bunny said. "I'll bring something the doctor gave me for my knee."

I hear myself agreeing to this; I didn't care what was brought, I would take it and my mother would come tomorrow. She would stay here until I was better and N came to his senses. Bunny would sleep in the guest room, and be available to A at all times to create a false feeling of normalcy and routine. Ron would stay home and mind the grandparental fort. This was all understood, although we had never rehearsed. Yet I didn't even have an extra key to give my mother. I would give Bunny my key. I would not be leaving the house, I reasoned. No one was leaving the house ever again.

Bushwhacked, I examined my hands. Same hands. Rings still there but no longer valid. Same trembling Kate Hepburn thing happening, but without the elegance. My mind floats like ash. I blame myself most cruelly. We should have had a master plan of some kind, as in an earthquake. N and I live on a major fault line, the San Andreas, a fact now sharply significant. California, the Golden State with a divorce rate bubbling along at 58 percent. The long and deep fault line splitting the bedrock, spreading with the brisk rate of dissolution down toward Los Angeles, just a few hundred miles south: home of the La Brea Tar Pits, Disneyland, Loma Prieta, Hollywood. All of this ricocheting across the nation to New York and back again, exploding in a quasar of terrorism and cultural disintegration. The velocity of doom seemed quite high, an obvious, palpable pall over the entire state and the country as well.

I should have seen this coming, and left N first. Gone on religious sabbatical, Outward Bound, Vietnam, something. It seemed a great deal of people were going to Vietnam.

"Are you certain you don't want me to come over right now?" Bunny broke the silence.

"No. I'll be all right tonight."

I was very far from all right, far enough for it not to matter if Bunny came over or not. In point of fact, I needed this night to have a complete yet finite and private nervous breakdown. I actually thought this might be possible. A was asleep: *Well. A miracle already,* I thought. He had slept through his father leaving. He would not even remember this night.

Something in my neck tightened. I stood up and went to the

freezer, extracting the pack of Winston Lights I'd stored there since we were trying to get pregnant and I had quit smoking. I open the pack with my teeth.

I have a new mantra, which I chant softly to myself: "Oh My God Oh My God."

I take a bottle of aspirin and a tumbler of mandarin-flavored vodka into the attic guest loft along with the cigarettes. I didn't know it then, but I was setting up camp, retrenching until I could ascertain my next move. How to continue.

I didn't think this would happen to me, I didn't think it could happen to me, I don't want it to happen to me.

Any way I slice reality it comes out poorly, and I feel an urge to not exist, something I have never felt before; and now here it comes with conviction, almost panic. I mentally bless and exonerate anyone who has kicked a chair out from beneath them or swallowed opium in large chunks. My mind has met their environment, here in the void. I understand perfectly.

In the vicinity of his bureau, I notice that he has left his martini glass with the three olives on the floor. That isn't like him. N loves to eat garnish, all forms of garnish. Is it a sign?

I eat the three olives, sucking the vodka from each one. I drink fresh vodka from his glass, neat. It is the last act I fully remember before I pass out naked on the futon, a full ashtray at both ends.

Good for Charlie

My mother sweeps into the house with all the majesty of a barrister. I can almost hear the air start to move again. Bunny is wearing a poncho made of orange pleather and stretch pants with stirrups that disappear into sling-back pumps. Her purse means business; it is the extra-large duffel from Coach with the tags that jingle like spurs. From her purse she extracts a fifth of Jack Daniel's and places it on the living room table; also a half gallon of butter pecan ice cream, which is whisked into the freezer as she roots about for snifters. It is nine thirty in the morning.

"Do you have any peanuts?" Bunny asks brightly, carefully emptying an ashtray into a can of duck fat that N had been saving for something really special. He loves to cook for special occasions, many of which involve clients or potential clients, which is anyone with tech skills or money or both.

"No," I say. "I don't have any peanuts."

"I see," Bunny says, squinting into the refrigerator. "We're going to have to make a trip to the store."

We all go to the store. I walk behind my mother and son with the slump of the defeated and the abandoned. I look at all the food, the army of overstuffed carts packed full of Economy sizes of everything, huge sacks of mesquite coals, and red meat Value Packs displaying six fat steaks on a white tray. These people know where their husbands are. I would like to vomit. I would like to vomit my soul out.

Bunny piles anything that has no nutritional value into the shopping cart. Raspberry Zingers, bacon marbled with fat, sausage patties, Dr Pepper, frozen latkes, sour cream, whipped cream, half-and-half, coffee, doughnuts, potato chips, French onion dip, cookies, frozen turnovers, and, in a moment of weakness, a bag of fresh avocados.

"Can you think of anything else you need?"

"A rope," I say.

Bunny gives me a look and then hands over *The National Enquirer*, saying, "Read this. Charlie Sheen is getting another divorce."

"Yes. We're like twins, Mom. Charlie and me. We're like *this*," I say, holding up two straight fingers pressed close together.

I step away, examine a package of edamame. I look at the expiration date: today. Why is edamame always ready to expire? It's so urgent for a vegetable. Edamame. It sounds like an assisted form of suicide. Is there an advertising concept in this? I wonder, trying to focus on something tangible. My frequent work as a freelance copywriter strays rather far from the realm of soy, but one never knows. Here in Marin, organically farmed vegetables are worshipped as cats were once worshipped in Egypt. I have found that people who feel strongly about organic vegetables and fruit are likely to be very, very angry.

I pick up an artichoke, $2.49, organic. It looks bitter. You can tell, the leaves are trying to get away from the thing itself, they curl outward. I have been an estranged wife for one day and already I have been warned against becoming bitter; I was told this immediately by a close friend whom I formerly thought of as sane. Upon regaining consciousness this morning, and after giving A a hideously cheerful breakfast? *That* was my emergency-girlfriend-telephone-call reward:

Don't get bitter.

"Help me with these groceries, honey," Bunny says, getting into the front seat of her car and turning on the radio to KABL, where Sinatra is singing "Summer Wind." I load the six bags of groceries into the back of my mother's Chrysler LeBaron while Bunny slams the empty shopping cart back into its corral.

N always used to load the groceries on Saturdays, I think. Already things are changing, it's starting with small shit but oh it's starting, the change, the irrevocable impossible change. The divorce concept seems to be something I am carrying around under my coat, keeping to myself and so afraid to look at, a human head in a hatbox. The whole world seems tilted, my inner ear displaced by a hole where my spouse used to be.

"Technology is full of holes," N always says.

Eyes

It was my eyes that had drawn N. I know this. His first word on being introduced to me was, "Wonderful."

Some genetic mutation, my eyes are wide-set and almost crossed, but in such agreement so as to startle. As a child I had been teased, had wished I could change them with a wand. Later I had used my eyes mostly to attract; this had lessened my insight into men. I saw my reflection in their eyes, but not the men themselves, not clearly. This preserved the idea that all intelligent and even vaguely attractive men were essentially good. Delusion detests focus and romance provides the veil.

N revealed his name and spoke the one word, reaching out his hand with such immediate pleasure that I felt we had met before and I hadn't remembered. This being San Francisco, everyone seemed to be from somewhere else altogether. He wore neat jeans with a black T-shirt and good soft leather shoes and thin socks and a stylish but unobtrusive watch. He could have been from any-where, which was very alluring. I didn't want to know, thought it might be enough just to lightly hold hands until I had regained my bearings and prepared myself in some way for this encounter.

"Wonderful": such an active word, to be full of wonder. He tossed some other truths, about media and Apple. He suggested I invest in Yahoo! at our first crossing; I regret to say I didn't. He never said I told you so. It seemed he was a kind of pedestrian prophet, doling out droll information in nice pieces. A genius at accessorizing and conversation, a man of few but precise words; he would select them as instruments for edification and union.

My last boyfriend, James, had spoken rapidly and often; his words had filled the air with dense molecules. It was like being in a crowd, being with James. Whereas, from the very begin-ning, being with N was very much like being alone, enhanced by low, resonant syllables. In this way we slid at once down the chute of mutual consent.

I remember how pleased I felt when N did speak at any length. It was not a torrent of dewy revelations and difficult questions; it was a nice sprinkling of words. Only his eyes and hands moved, he was fully contained. We both refused the hors d'oeuvres and fell silent when Rostropovich came on the stereo. For small reasons we took to each other like urchin children. It had all seemed as inevitable as sunset. Instead it was the beauty of the sun glinting upon the scythe.

Man Swears to God

It was April Fools' Day when my husband came to pick up his clothes. I had the bizarre feeling that it might, in the very final analysis, be some kind of elaborate prank. That for a man so thoughtful and precise to do this on April Fools' meant he was not entirely serious about this divorce.

I look at our bed, his leather garment bag spread across it like a prostitute. N once recited the entire text from "The Love Song of J. Alfred Prufrock" to me on that same bed. I remember the boxers he was wearing. Blue paisley.

As he packs his best clothes into his luggage, I can't seem to tear my eyes away. I need him to tell me if there is another woman in his life, someone important and close at hand.

"Don't make me hear it from someone else," I beg. "PLEASE

spare me that humiliation. Show me that modicum of respect."

"No, I swear it's untrue," N said, choosing socks.

Our son toddles over to N's luggage and tosses his knotty doll in. N tosses the doll out and snaps his suitcase shut. He winces and hobbles upstairs with what looks like extreme suffering, and probably is.

Crazy

I am sure N will come back. He has not yet done so. There has been no male footfall on the porch, heavy and meaningful. Such leaden silence has an actual sound, the sound of disappearance. I register daily this absence of hard shoes bustling across the dry redwood planks, the porch where so recently he stood at our doorway, poised to leave us.

How can he not come back?

This is much worse than losing a cat. You do not wish the cat dead, for example, after the first two days. You still love the cat and presumably the cat still loves you, or some variation of love that may in fact be dependence and even indifference. People should be informed, as adopting a cat and becoming married take about the same amount of time and money and yet have such drastically different results. Indeed, except for the similar price ($28) and the average time spent together, all similarity between pet adoption and marriage ends nastily.

I am going crazy, and no one can help me. This is what really happens to wives who are left with small children. I never fully appreciated this fact before.

Conversely, I thought humiliation would be everything, but it's such a nothing. When his friends call (he has told virtually no one), I say simply, "He left me. Here is his number at work." If they probe, I will give them a few random details. It depends on my mood; it is like choosing shoes for that day, or earrings.

I send his mother, Françoise, the green silk scarf from Joan & David that I discovered weeks ago, which N claims he bought for me. But it was the wrong color. I never wear green, it sallows my complexion.

Françoise calls to thank me, thrilled and solicitous.

"You're very welcome," I say, crushing out a cigarette in an ashtray from the Fairmont. First anniversary.

He is bitter because our best friends, Lisa and Eric, are siding with me. We all used to be part of a tight, exhilarant posse of loose adults and sweet, funny children.

When she heard the news, Lisa called me immediately. "Tell me everything over lunch tomorrow. I already know he's in the wrong."

Traditionally in this native land, when a member of the tribe betrays, the tribe turn their back on him.

Harvested Raw from the Ocean

I look forward to lunch with Lisa, though she is always an hour late, and everyone plans around her. She runs a marketing department, which provides her with a nice living and enough money to refuse everyone who doesn't meet her requirements.

As Lisa walks into Aqua, a place where people willingly spend up to $150 for something raw harvested from the ocean, she is wearing a white 1960s Pucci mini wedding dress and talking to herself, wearing her cell phone headset. In her black-gloved hands is a cup from Jack in the Box with a straw, through which I know Lisa is drinking Pepsi. Always Pepsi, never Coke, not even if we are in Mexico and that's all they have except tap water.

This is what knowing Lisa requires: patience.

Upon reaching the table, she terminates the call immediately, making a small cutting motion in the air.

"I'd ask you how you are, but I already know. You look like the wrath of God." Lisa settles into her seat, all ninety-five pounds of her.

"That's how I feel exactly," I say, watching as the waiter hovers nearby anxiously. Despite being petite, Lisa makes people fearful.

"Doll," Lisa says, "you have no idea how I have longed for this day."

"Do you really hate N that much now?"

"Your husband is a charismatic, good-looking man but of no real consequence. No: I love *you* that much. And look at you. He's practically sucked out all your blood."

I feel very pleased and also abashed, since Lisa almost never says anything against N. I hope Lisa doesn't feel sorry for me, I honestly can't think of anything worse at this moment. I wonder how backed up the bar is.

"I'm going to tell you something right now that is going to make you embrace this divorce as you never thought possible," Lisa says, leaning forward to show the half-moons of her small, sculpted breasts, and then takes a long dramatic pull on an imaginary cigarette.

"He was dating around while you two were courting."

"Really?"

"For a while," Lisa says.

I notice that I do not react as I ought to to this news. I suspected this transgression, in the back of my mind. Still, I didn't really know. Now I know. I feel angry but not homicidal; this may be unlooked-for progress. It may be that what has recently happened automatically trumps anything that has happened in the past.

"I knew that," I say, smiling and nodding as though at a good line in a play.

"Women were on him like lint," Lisa says, smoothing her skirt.

"But I didn't *know* know," I add, blotting my lips with my napkin. The waiters smash ice nearby, for the oysters.

"I am sorry. But you do know what this means."

"Yes. I do," I say. "It means it's worse than I thought. More widespread."

"No. It means it is much better than you thought. You see, your husband is a squirrel. He has always been a squirrel."

"And?"

"And now you are free of him, and you get A as a bonus prize."

"No. I'm sure it's going to be Joint Custody," I say.

"Trust me. The mother gets the child. Cheers," Lisa says, raising a glass of champagne that she somehow summoned without anyone appearing to notice.

"Cheers," I say, savoring the good champagne. "Remind me again of why I am well rid of him. . . ."

"All right, but then we must talk about something more gratifying.

"Hmmmm," Lisa continues, *"your husband."* This time a bit louder, recalling his file in her mental dossier, as though he weren't well known to her.

"May I help you?" Our waiter, a robust young man with a handsome face and a look of quiet despair, thinks that perhaps she has alerted him.

"Oh, I very much doubt that," Lisa says, smiling a brilliant smile at him until he backs away.

"Well. He has been a smart, charming man-child for as long as I have known him. That would be seven years now. But. The moment he hit fifty, he began to, I don't know . . . *curdle.*"

I butter a piece of bread, rapt.

"And in all that time, he never once treated me as if I were off the menu. It flattered me. I never thought he was serious; I'm not his type. No. No . . . ," she says, unfolding her napkin onto her white lap.

"What I object to is his sporadic lack of honesty and the fact that no matter how much he gives to Society and Third World Children, he would step over his own grandmother for skirt. There. I've said it, and now you can tell me all the details of how he left. I'm dying to know."

"This is going to take at least six courses," I say.

"Start at the beginning," Lisa says.

"Like I know where that is," I say, my eyes rolling up.

Yet maybe if I try very hard, I can remember. I can begin to make sense.

Clues

People told me not to get married; I didn't listen. No one ever listens, it seems to me now. Perhaps people should stop trying to communicate. N was not a communicator; early on, I'd insisted on communication. Now I see his point acutely. I would love to have him back to not communicate with me. I would never ask for communication again, I would simply go elsewhere for the deep fish. Also, I'm not at all sure I want to hear what he has to say, in this new vista. This works out well.

Long ago, my friend Christian, who lives in L.A., returned an entire letter to me, one I'd written announcing my engagement to be married. At the bottom of the page, Christian had scrawled the words DO NOT DO WHAT I SHOULD NOT HAVE DONE in red ink. Then he stuffed it in its old envelope and mailed it back. This was Christian's equivalent of a flare. He is a network executive and very sensitive as to what gets written down—nothing. He puts everything through a shredder, including paper towels.

Christian has an ex wife who lives in luxury on the interest of what he sends her every month in alimony. Anita has sequestered herself on an island in the Bahamas and will never remarry.

Christian has the alimony deducted from his pay stub so that he never sees it.

"If I see it," he says, "I could fall backwards dead."

After the settlement was final with Anita, Christian marched into Tiffany's and said to the manager, *If you ever see me in here again, I want you to call the police and have me arrested and sent to an Appalachian prison where I would be buggered up the ass. Because I would rather have that happen than get married again.*

N is a good man. An example of this would be, he delivers toys to hospitalized children twice yearly. He also walks on the outside of the street when we are walking together. If there is a regular apple and a bruised apple, he will give me the regular apple and not call attention to it. But then he left me, betraying me in spirit and body, and did not call attention to it.

There were signs at the end: He would wake up in a sweat, before dawn. I would hear his quick, shallow breathing as I lay motionless beside him. I played possum. I did this, as the possum does, out of fear.

There appeared in our home a lovely small hardcover book of Zen·Poetry with a feminine, curvaceous inscription "To N xo Me." I'd never seen it before, hadn't ordered it online. It was a rogue book. I looked at the inscription for a whole minute; read it three times. Closed the book. Vomited in my half-bathroom. Afterward, I brushed my teeth and threw the book away in the Trash Master.

N didn't seem to miss it.

Who is the Zen Poetry Book Woman? Somehow I know it is not a simple acquaintance or a lover of books who is happily married to another lover of books. It is something else. The curliness of her handwriting oozed sexuality; the X and O teemed with familiarity.

I think: I would like to take N back to a store right now, like a rake.

I would say, "Oh, this rake is uneven. Do you have any where the tines go straight across?"

I would like to do a straight exchange.

But there are things that cannot be returned. Errant husbands are one of them. Wives are not. Wives can be exchanged; I have always known this. I thought I had an exemption in boundlessly loving N and our son, giving money to a home for battered women and children, and contributing to the Redwood Gospel Mission. I was wrong.

Magic Stones

I travel back in time, falling back into what I know for certain, the historical data I cling to in order to not go mad, not assume I made a suicidal and well-informed error in marrying this man.

When we were first married, I thought to surprise my husband with an overnight stay at Stinson Beach, booking the very last room in the area, after many phone calls. A little bed-and-breakfast called the Redwood Inn, only a block from the beach.

We say nothing to each other, but walk to the fog-drenched beach immediately. I am having a terribly stressful time at the ad agency, one of the worst times I can recall having. I am possibly about to be fired from my job. Some time has to pass before I know; the suspense seems unbearable. On the beach, N starts collecting the small, smooth stones along the water's edge. He wants them for the cactus he has just gotten for our kitchen; he wants to line the cactus pot with stones. When he brings them back, we look at them, spread out on the blanket. It is an increasingly overcast day.

I count them; there are thirty-two stones. I start absentmindedly stacking them up in small piles, like tiny sculptures. I do this for a while and then after about twenty minutes, joke about how I may want to keep the stones, maybe.

He says, "Okay. They'll be your magic stones . . . and whenever you're worried, you can stack them and then everything will get better. I'll buy you a wooden cigar box to put them in."

A week later he brought me the cigar box.

Not everyone can make stones magic. Hardly anyone will even try.

The Morning-After Pill

Not long after he filed the divorce petition, I had sex with N. It was extremely passionate, as though we intend to swallow each other whole.

"I don't have the right," he said, pulling down his boxers. "I don't deserve to."

"That's true," I said, lifting my nightgown up and off. I needed his skin on mine.

"I don't want to be a hypocrite," he said.

"You are a hypocrite," I replied. "We all are."

Afterward the room was full with an electric silence, a sort of eloquent lie. I asked the air, *"Didn't you expect this would happen?"*

"No," N said, with a perplexed look on his face, as though he'd found a quarter inside his ear.

"Well, I did," I said.

What was he doing at the house at seven a.m.? I'd tricked him by claiming A was sick when he wasn't. Upon N's arrival, I saw he had dressed himself in some worn jeans and a soft flannel shirt. Flannel shirts should be outlawed for ex husbands; I realize this now. Flannel shirts are to women what crotchless panties are to men. I was wearing a silk chemise the color of persimmons.

Later I showed him to the door. "You have to go. I might not be myself very soon."

He left a bit too easily and with obvious relief. His feet were swift and sure on the muddy path.

I called Lisa. "It's the last time," I said. "This was the last time we'll sleep together."

"All right," Lisa said. "Good." She hung up, as if to finalize it without any caveats sneaking in from my side of the telephone.

I debrief Bunny over tea while A sleeps, having had his traditional bedtime snack of cheddar cheese and cold green apple wedges.

I feel bad, as though I had formerly been two years' sober. The abandonment came, and now this shabby bacchanal. Bunny is playing gin rummy with me, perched at the table in a Chanel knockoff, barefooted. I am sliding out of my jeans and T-shirt, having lost some weight.

"I just wanted to make a connection," I explain.

"Well, you've certainly done that." Bunny sighs, holding a card in the air. "It's inevitable. Just let it pass . . . like a virus. . . ."

"There's something else," I say.

"What?" Bunny asks. "Was he impotent?" Bunny has a frisson of glee in her voice.

"I'm off the Pill," I say.

Bunny cocks an eyebrow.

"I can't get pregnant, Mom. It would be like a hole in one. I cannot be getting pregnant this late in the game."

"Generations have . . . ," my mother says.

"And why would I be on the Pill now, because it's not like I'm going to sleep with anyone." Except—it would seem—my soon-to-be-ex husband.

"Consider stocking the morning-after pill," Bunny intones, laying her cards faceup. "Gin."

Cocktail Napkin

I discovered the cocktail napkin on the floor of the nursery when I was eight months pregnant. The lyrics to a love song by Cole Porter, in my husband's crabbed handwriting, on the back of a napkin from Café Claude. I was organizing the baby's room when I saw it on the floor. I read the words as I straightened up. The lyrics were erotic, tender. By their context, it was clear that these words were not for me; also I see he has scrawled someone's name a few times, in various margins of the napkin. The name was not Suzanne; I couldn't quite make it out.

When he came home, I held the cocktail napkin high overhead. The first thing he did was cross the room and grab the napkin out of my hand as though it were incendiary. He flew across the room with vampire speed; his right arm shot out and snatched the thin paper away, as though it could blow my hand off. Then he tore it up, threw it into the blazing fireplace, and wiped his brow with his handkerchief; it was all very smooth and sophisticated, very *Masterpiece Theatre*.

I should have known then it wasn't *nothing*, as he called it. But I was eight months pregnant. No sense closing the barn door now, or so I thought. I swallowed the *nothing*, straightaway after the usual tears and denial.

It should be mentioned that I adored N; I thought his approval necessary to drawing a clear breath, his arms the place where all healing took place. That the first time I saw him I felt an electrical surge, and knew that he was something to me. That the second time we met, I knew he was someone I could marry. That the third time we met, I knew he was the only man I wanted to marry, and that I would do anything in my power to obtain his presence. And I did. I did anything. In this attack mode of behavior, I was not so different from a mistress.

I sensed he may have occasionally strayed in some of his past relationships. It was something I felt but ignored, a rent in the fabric of an otherwise splendid garment I thought I could mend. I thought I could live with it—I thought, yes and I admit it, that I would be different. That at the very least, middle age and children would slow him down; however, they seemed to accelerate his pace.

Three years into the fat of the marriage, he stopped calling me during the day. He'd not be available at his office between twelve noon and three o'clock in the afternoon—long lunches.

N came home one day wearing a different shirt from the white polo sweater he'd left the house with; he sashayed in sporting a fine new fitted Brooks Brothers shirt, unbuttoned to expose the very top of his chest hair. N said he had gotten black ink on his sweater. When the sweater came home the next day, there was no ink. He claimed a coworker removed the stain with Zout.

"That Zout is really something," he said. I agreed it was.

Three and a half years into the marriage, he started calling me Baby, instead of my name, as if he were Jackie Gleason. He was withdrawn. His cell phone would ring and he would swiftly answer and say, *I'll call you back*, and hang up with a silly smile about who it was; I never asked, he had taught me not to ask. He would get furious if I asked him where he was going or where he had been. He told me I was not a wife, more of a prison warden. He pointed to the importance of his work and the privacy of his clients.

Whenever he woke up suddenly, he was visibly startled to see me at his side.

Soon he was online every night until one or two a.m. Often he would wake up at three or four a.m. and go back online. He would shut down the computer screen when I walked in. In the past, he used to take the laptop to bed with him and we would both be on our laptops, hips touching. He stopped doing that, slipping off to his office instead and closing the door even when A was asleep. He started closing doors behind him. I was steeped in denial, but my body knew.

Depression followed; I was furtive, secretly bedridden in its grip. But a man like N sees. You can't get anything past technology writers. Their business is facts and images, their minute distinctions and vicissitudes.

Did he care? He did, he cared deeply. He held my hand and spoke in paternal tones and urged me to go to my doctor and obtain antidepressant and antianxiety medication. He researched the medication and conferred with my doctor regarding dosage. He was efficient and thorough. Although if I play devil's advocate, I'll venture that he didn't want his wife to be in the loony bin when he made his escape.

Follow the Pfizer pill road!
Follow the Pfizer pill road!
Follow, follow, follow, follow,
Follow the Pfizer pill road!

The Talk

More days pass. I sit for hours, drinking water and smoking in the same chair. Bunny says nothing, just nods with silent approbation from the couch: a mother who is watching her child doing homework. She reads the newspaper, eats a bowl of cereal for dinner. Makes tea, drinks it alone, watching me with a sidelong look as I pass her on the way to the bathroom. I am all cheekbones and eyes, the weight still sliding off. Bunny surveys me and sighs.

"I never looked better than when your father left me. I was down to an eight."

We have scheduled the talk with A about the divorce today. Bunny is with me and A in the kitchen for moral support and also for the box of giant warm Cinnabons that she has brought. There is no etiquette for this.

I think, *It's a little song about abandonment, and it goes something like this. . . .*

I wish I had a guitar, some sort of happy prop. I have nothing. Just me. This is how it's going to be from now on; I am not nearly enough, and I am disappearing pound by pound. I'll end up a pile of black clothes and a witch hat on the floor.

"Do you remember when your daddy lived here?" I begin.

"Yes." A gauges the room. Then he sighs in exhaustion, as if he is being asked to play Tuptim in *The King and I* for the six hundredth time.

"I know my daddy doesn't live here anymore," he says.

"Of course," I say. "Yes. But he still loves you very, very much. You are still his Boy."

"I know that," A says.

"Do you still love Daddy?" I ask, and suddenly look over at Bunny, as if to say, *Help me, I am going off script*. Bunny shrugs.

A says, "I love Daddy."

I feel odd relief, as though it is my love for A that was in question, or something just as precious. I also know that whatever is said here, there will be damage.

"Do you have anything you want to ask me? Anything about your daddy or mommy or how you feel?" I chirrup.

Bunny coughs.

"What?" I ask, defensive.

Bunny leans forward and whispers into my ear: "I have a Neurosis behind my back, can you guess what it is? I think you're through talking now. I hope that you are."

Then A asks, "Why?"

"Why?" I say. "Why is always a good question. Well, I'll tell you why. Of course, it's not your fault, you know that right?"

"Sure, sure."

"Well . . . let's ask Grandma . . . what is that thing when a man decides he would be, um . . . you know . . . more Himself, and, well . . . this means he may want to live on his own? What is that thing?"

"Ambivalence?" Bunny suggests.

"Yes," I say. "We had too much of that."

We all consider this.

A says, "But do you still love Daddy and does Daddy still love you?"

I am startled. There is no good answer here. This is from out of the sky.

"Yes, my darling boy. Everyone loves everyone. Eat your Rice Krispies," Bunny says, her voice calm, a decoy.

I look away out the front window. Look back. Nobody has disappeared. And I have to do it; I have to say something resembling the truth. Fatigue pulls at my limbs with a relentless pressure.

"Yes is not exactly true, son. In fact I don't know what's true. But when I find out, I'll tell you."

"Chocolate milk!" he cries, as if a difficult code has been cracked and the prize is chocolate milk. He runs from the kitchen. I look back at my mother, who is calmly slicing a cinnamon roll into quarters.

I ask, "Do you know what's true?"

Bunny says, "I know what used to be true. But no, I don't know what is true now."

"That's what I thought," I say, arranging myself facedown on the linoleum.

"We don't know who N is anymore," Bunny says.

"I know," I say, my head turned sideways. "It's as though he's dead. Or I am. Do I get to choose? A person should get to choose."

"I know one thing about men," Bunny says with finality, leaving the room to check on A. "They never die when you want them to."

Paraguay

I put the wedding album in N's empty underwear drawer, as though it belonged only to him, a kind of peccadillo. A week or so later I display it on the coffee table for all to see. I want to own this transition, to not simply swallow the shame of it entire. I will push for every little irony. If he looks at it, there's a slim chance that he could change his mind. They really are extraordinary photographs, I feel. It is true that he never took much of an interest. But maybe now he will, a kind of Retrospective poignancy could overtake him. Can this end well? I am willing to do anything to make it feel as though we are still married, that he still loves me. Yet it is with great reluctance that I sense what is most likely coming. The pit. The lonely single-mother one-income tar pit.

Although N is paying half the mortgage, I promptly apply for a credit line on our home and extensively document my earnings, just in case. My own personal savings of $12,000 have started to take on a magisterial glow, the scepter to a life that may be my own; and may not include living out of my car and rickets. I remember the anxiety I faced quitting my full-time advertising job when A was born; now I stare it down once more. I will cannibalize the house with impunity. The equity loan will meet the household expenses through the year. I can switch to an interest-only ARM loan that will slice our mortgage in half; after A has graduated high school, I can slide gracefully into a soft bankruptcy. In a dozen or so years, none of the principle on the house will be paid off, but technically I will still own it. Meanwhile I can be a freelance copywriter, saying yes to everything I am asked to write, including newspaper coupons for high-fiber cereal, Brazilian tampon print ads, and ads for miraculous yet noninvasive cosmetic products for women age thirty-five to fifty-five. I will advertise my way out of the tar pit. I don't need to be sane to write claims for waterproof mascara, or happy. I can simply describe products and services that people don't really need and make them want them.

After this year, let the chips fall. Who knows what could happen. Look, I reasoned, at what has already happened.

"Why don't you come home?" I wrote to N in a tragically humiliating e-mail last night.

"I can't, now," he replied, to my mind implying that there may be a future time when this same offer might be good. Adroit, his comment was saving him from even this final commitment of severance.

"What do you miss about me?" I wrote.

I have the nagging suspicion that he is not truly leaving us, but is on vacation.

"Your presence," he answers.

They ought to do away with divorce settlements. Instead, both parties should flip a coin. The winner gets to stay where he or she is and keep everything. The loser goes to Paraguay. That's it.

Patricia Arquette

Daily I walk around my small, picturesque town with a thought bubble over my head: Person Going Through A Divorce. When I look at other people, I automatically form thought bubbles over their heads. Happy Couple With Stroller. Innocent Teenage Girl With Her Whole Life Ahead Of Her. Content Grandmother And Grandfather Visiting Town Where Their Grandchildren

Live With Intact Parents. Secure Housewife With Big Diamond. Undamaged Group Of Young Men On Skateboards. Good Man With Baby In BabyBjörn Who Loves His Wife. Dogs Who Never Have To Worry. Young Kids Kissing Publicly. Then every so often I see one like me, one of the shambling gaunt women without makeup, looking older than she is: *Divorcing Woman Wondering How The Fuck This Happened.*

Since all of this began, I have lost twenty-six pounds. I can wear a size six bikini again. It is a benefit. I chalk it up. When people see me, they say, "You look great!"

"My husband left me," I say gaily.

They say, "Oh, no."

"Oh, yes," I say.

I have slimmed down because I do not eat, having recently discovered that it is a largely superfluous activity that grief and/or shock cancels out. When I do eat, it is things like Sugar Babies and Cheetos. I have two Chips Ahoy! cookies at the end of each day: my reward for not hanging myself with a bra in the garage.

I am also saving scads of money at the supermarket. I buy no meat, no thick steaks or pork chops or turkey basil sausages. My refrigerator is still crammed with condiments, meat and condiments being the mainstay of most men. But I have no man now. I am like a movie: *No Man Of Her Own.*

I feel halved, and something else which I cannot quite admit to myself: giddy.

On an inspiration, I have my engagement ring sized to a pinky ring, returning to the man who originally sold it to us.

I remove my sunglasses and look him straight in the eye as I place the diamond ring on a flat, black velvet cushion.

"Can you size this to my pinky finger," I say. It is not a question.

Without missing a beat, he says, "Are you sure you don't want to make it into a pendant?"

This is not his first divorce.

"I don't wear pendants," I say.

"You look great," he says.

"Thank you," I say.

I know it is true. Knowing this keeps my head high as I walk out with a small yellow jewelry receipt. As I leave the store and enter the street, I begin to sob. I feel very strong that I waited until I was out on the street, where no one knows me, where no other couples are picking out their wedding bands, so happy, so innocent.

For a while, I took a small pleasure out of the fact that someone was divorcing Patricia Arquette. If Patricia Arquette is getting divorced, a woman who is stunning and sexy and smart besides, then maybe this whole thing is all right.

Two nights later, when I watch *Entertainment Tonight*, their cover story is: Arquette's Husband Withdraws Petition for Divorce.

"Fuck," I say.

I am drunk in front of the television, chain-smoking. I have not bathed in two days. Still, I had identified with Patricia Arquette. But that's all over now.

Transience

A packs his Elmo bottle holder in a paper bag, along with a single Goldfish cracker. His fine brown hair is bunched up on his head in a topknot.

"Bye," he says.

"Good-bye," I say.

His first word was Duh Duh. That's what he calls N: Duh Duh. Then he went on to say Duck and then, Mama. I didn't mind being third. When he was born, I was under general anesthesia, so it was N who ushered him into the world for the first two hours. I didn't mind this, either; it made the birth feel fully integrated between mother and father. Ron took photos through the nursery window of N holding A up with a stunning smile of pride and relief.

"See you soon," A says now, swinging his bag of travel essentials as he toddles toward the door.

"Fine!"

This is much easier than when N left. Our son is unable to grasp and simultaneously turn doorknobs yet. If only this trick could be unlearned by men over thirty, many more families would celebrate Christmas together.

I have many wishes and most of them are impossible. Irony angles in from all directions: Lately, for no reason I can ascertain, A sings "Ashes, Ashes, All Fall Down" when we're driving around town. It is so poignant and sad; I want to scream in the moving car. I want to run down a few squirrels.

Ashes, ashes, all fall down.

When I woke up this morning, Sunday, I began to cry, a slow trickle out of my right eye like warm butter. I am disgusted with myself. Sunday is just like any other day. It is. It should be. It isn't.

I call N and leave one message: "It's hard not to hate you. How could you?" I inquire.

And I honestly don't know. It's like watching someone do a triple backflip dismount and land on two feet, solid, arms splayed in the air. I know I could never do it, don't even know where I would begin to learn, but some people are built for it. He was handcrafted to leave, had practiced on other women since adolescence. I was one of an unnumbered series.

Meanwhile, my diamond pinky ring keeps slipping off.

"It doesn't want to be worn," Bunny says.

"It proves to me that I was once loved," I say.

"You are loved. You don't need to prove it."

I need to have it sized down to a four. But can I face jewelry salesman Roger again, and the couples choosing bands, couples who are marching straight into the maw of connubial hell? I decide that I can't. I wrap a tiny piece of tape around the ring to make it fit.

Blown

Last night N and I went out for Mexican food with our son. We play Family. We drive right through town just like before. Except N is going back to my house to take a truckful of boxes of his belongings. I help him with the boxes while A laughs and capers, soon running inside to watch *SpongeBob SquarePants*. N takes only a few of the boxes, I note with satisfaction. I wonder what other strange things are happening in garages across America. This cannot be the only Twilight Garage.

"It's sad . . . ," I say to him, lighting a cigarette, which I know he hates. Suddenly I don't care. Let him breathe deeply of my secondhand smoke. He nods and walks to his SUV, his Cuisinart cradled to his chest. I've blown it, the whole grisly charade. I am a bad wife, soon to be a non-wife.

I have to run out to him, he has left his computer bag next to the big chair in the living room—as he used to do, as if he still lives here.

"Thanks," he says, shouldering it. He climbs back in his car and drives away. I listen to the distinctive sound of his car.

Now I look for my son's nail clippers and I find a picture that somehow hasn't made its way to the storeroom with the other war crime evidence and wedding photos and such. It's a photograph of N holding up our son at six months old. A wore a green romper, the sun slanting across their upraised similar faces.

I call him at work to ask him if he remembers that picture. "I do," he says.

"No, you don't," I say. "You couldn't."

"Yes, I do," he asserts.

I look at it and cry and ask him: "Why. Why."

He tells me how well I am doing, what I am going to become; I say *I don't care what I am going to become. I want to be what we were. A family.*

"It was so brief," I say.

Was it a dream? I think. It is possible I dreamt it. The wedding, everything. That was another life, a different woman; this one is thinner, wiser, this one has bangs and a toddler and two mortgages. This one is not waking up.

Gains

There is no man in the house that I have to try and make happy. There are no more arguments, or nights when I turn away from N in quiet despair as he snores with an entitled regularity. Everything also stays cleaner; the toilet seat is perpetually down. I have the remote control to the television; no one can take that away. I can watch the Lifetime channel without derision.

Also, I can let myself go. Unfortunately I am not a serious or dedicated drinker and cannot hang from chandeliers, intoxicated with my own hilarity . . . but at night when my son is asleep, I can smoke again. Smoking again seems to be the major benefit to divorce, so far. I must say the benefits do not begin to rival the benefits of marriage yet, but it is early. I try to withhold judgment. I cry now, a bit every day. This, of course, is not a benefit. But it's the only way I know to feel better.

So many events and moments that seemed insignificant add up. I remember how for the last Valentine's Day, N gave flowers but no card. In restaurants, he looked off into the middle distance while my hand would creep across the table to hold his. He would always let go first. I realize I can't remember his last spontaneous gesture of affection.

I read poetry, Theodore Roethke.

"In a dark time, the eye begins to see . . ."

I do see a bit more. I remember one desolate Sunday night, wondering: Is this how I'm going to spend the rest of my life? Married to someone who is perpetually distracted and somewhat wistful, as though a marvelous party is going on in the next room, which but for me he could be attending?

I could probably find another man and remarry, if I wasn't still in love with N and if we weren't still legally married. Let's not any of us forget that for a second.

I decide not to read love poetry for a while.

Lockerbie

I am in my parents' hot tub with my mother.

"I guess two months probably isn't long enough to grieve," I say.

"No. It's going to be far more extensive. Two years minimum. You're not special," Bunny thoughtfully says. "I still grieve for your father, occasionally, and he's been dead twenty-five years. Or is it twenty-six?"

I ignore this, swaying in warm, bubbly water. I am an egg noodle in a vat of chicken stock, an organic carrot whose time has come. And I'm ready, I think. I've lived; I've been published. I've borne a child.

"Take me now, God!" I shout to the inky sky. "I'm ready."

"You're not ready. You're not even divorced yet," Bunny says. "You cannot die married to that man."

"I don't know how it all went so wrong so fast," I say, and begin to laugh uncontrollably. I know I am near hysteria.

"It DID," my mother affirms.

"One minute I'm eating salted peanuts and the cocktail cart is coming out? The next minute I'm hanging upside down and I can see the ground," I say.

"There's a finger in your drink, and it's not yours," Bunny muses.

"Fiery ball," I say of my exploding marriage. "Lockerbie."

Bunny adds, "People on the ground are killed."

"I see human torches. And one of them is N."

"There's an arm, lying next to a Samsonite cosmetic case," my mother enthuses. "And a doll. There should be a doll. Like in *Titanic*."

We cackle like *Macbeth* witches around a cauldron. We are missing the third witch, but it's all right. A is inside their house, asleep; he can be the third witch. He can be Honorary Witch.

I relax in the frantic bubbles. Steam wreathes our heads. Bunny directs me to the foot jets and the lumbar sprays in her über Jacuzzi, The Jet Set. She insists I need one of these spa Jacuzzis.

Especially now, she croons, as though I have not been divorced but rather stricken with polio. She says to call her first before I do anything, because she knows the staff. She is ceding her referral discount to me. Ten percent. It's so Good Samaritan of my mother.

I tell her about the anticipated Big Scene with N, wherein he begs forgiveness in my newly renovated house and I sit with my legs crossed, considering how to decline him, but in a nice way. I describe how A is also casual yet professional as he walks his daddy to the door.

I say to my mother: "A is looking at me with a mute question on his face, as if to say: *'What's my motivation?'*

"The master shot?" I say. "N on his knees in the driveway as I neatly shut the front door. Inside, A says, *'Bye-bye, Daddy! See you soon!'*"

"Through faint yet exquisite morning birdsong, you can hear your ex husband weeping," Bunny intones.

"Fantastic," I say.

"Well. You never know. The world is round," my mother majestically says. She is referring to N's spousal bad karma, which she feels certain is about to come in, like the mail.

"It is exceedingly round," I say.

"And getting rounder," Bunny says, reaching for another sip of Muscat.

Losses

As if to prove a secondary point, N calls late last night, boozy and expansive. He says of course he still loves me as a person, as the Mother of his Child, and he always will.

"I love you as the mother of my child": the kiss of death.

Mother of His Child: demotion. I am beginning to see this truism: Mothers are not always wives. I have been stripped of a piece of self.

He announces that lately, he keeps losing things. "Like your wife and child," I want to say, but don't. At forty, I've learned not to say everything clever, not to score every point. He now resides in Russian Hill, in what he describes as the hippest neighborhood in the city of San Francisco, the hippest he personally has ever lived in. It's only eighteen miles away, but it may as well be China. Our paths will never cross.

I say, "You know, it's probably very sick, but I like taking care of you. I like being married."

N claims he took care of me too, would sometimes take A so I could write, work. Yes. I remember he did that. I remember all the meals he cooked early on, during the hot summer of my pregnancy . . . the carefully constructed salads we would eat with our fingers in bed, the air-conditioning humming. The way he proposed to me all over again in a red-shuttered room on the main canal of Venice, when I was pregnant . . . how that proposal meant so much more than the first one, because I was carrying A and my neck had disappeared.

"We were a good team," I say. Knowing that we really weren't a good team, but we wanted to be. I wanted to be.

I hang up, crying.

"I miss Duh Duh," I say to A, because he has woken up and is staring at me as though I have a chopstick through my head. Sometimes I must admit to him the fact that I have feelings that could be construed as negative or sad. I am a whole person, one who bleeds. I am not the perfect galvanized-steel mother I would like to be. Meanwhile his father is off riding the manic dolphin to Valhalla.

My son has found his old pacifier under the bed, he hands it over. He always knows what to do. I put it in my mouth and suck. It feels marvelous. We trade it back and forth. I am laughing and crying. A finds the Mini Oreos under the bed; I let him eat several, until his mouth is black.

Fucking Holidays

"FUCKING holidays," Bunny says, after we discuss the issue of Mother's Day. I have agreed to have brunch with N. I just want to be honored as a mother. I don't want to be alone on Mother's Day. It just happens to be at the same restaurant we got engaged at. I know this is a clear case of masochism, know even as I go in that it is not really a warm shower, that I'm going to be gassed, choking for air and going down in a heap of flesh and bone and impeccable service.

Mother's Day at the Lark Creek Inn. I weep almost constantly throughout, as unobtrusively as possible. I tell N that if this were a movie, we would be able to spin time backwards and have a separate, happy ending. He digs into his Peach Soufflé French Toast and remarks that there was probably nothing I could have done to change anything. Inexplicably, he keeps taking pictures from a Leica camera that is slung around his neck. I ask him to take it off; I felt he was a journalist covering the scene: *A SORROWFUL YET POIGNANT SUBURBAN DIVORCE.* He takes the camera off.

I think, *There is the table where we got engaged. There is where we sat on my birthday, when I was pregnant. Upstairs is the special room where I threw a fiftieth birthday bash for him, hugely pregnant.* I know I am playing out some tragic Greek play and I'm horrified, but the show must go on. N starts to talk about his job.

I say, "I don't want to hear about your job." His job is not in the play.

I have dressed this way (white linen hat, filmy white dress, beige cashmere shawl he bought when we were engaged, cream opaque hosiery) for a reason: I want to look legitimate, to pass. I need to look like the other mothers. I am like them, only erased. I am in excruciating psychic pain and my eyes and nose run through every course (three), although the eggs Benedict are, as always, superlative.

I feel immediately better after N drops me off and leaves. I take A to the supermarket. A chortles when I swerve the cart wildly from side to side. When we come out to the parking lot, there is a great gust, and A lifts one arm into the air and shouts, "THE WIND, THE WIND."

I have lost practically nothing.

A Good Question

I am visiting my parents when suddenly Bunny removes her glasses and says, "I have to ask . . . is there someone else?"

"Where?" I ask.

Immediately after saying this, I realize that Bunny meant someone else N is involved with.

"No, I don't think so. He's home every night," I mumble.

"*Was* he?" Bunny prompts.

I must get the tense right. "He was home virtually every night, yes. And we were still having sex all the time . . . ," I rally.

"Well," Bunny says. She shoos a fly away from her pomegranate juice.

I say nothing further. My entire body, I notice, has gone tense as piano wire.

"If I were you," Bunny says, "I would prepare myself to find a third party involved in this. A woman may pop out of a closet. Be prepared, in case that happens."

"How would I do that?" I ask.

"Ah," Bunny says. "Well, you really can't. But you can at least consider the possibility as a valid one, and keep your mind open to that possibility."

"So . . . if I'm prepared, it won't hurt as much?"

Bunny says, "I can't guarantee that."

"What can you guarantee, O Nostradamus of Hayward?" I carp.

Bunny flashes her eyes at me. "I'm sixty-six years old. And if your husband isn't having an affair, well. I'd be very surprised."

I say, "I'm feeling hostile toward you now, Mom."

Bunny softens. "Honey. It's your choice. We don't have to talk about it."

"Well. It's nice to have one choice," I snipe. "Because I didn't choose any of this, you know. I was a good wife."

"Oh, I don't doubt that."

"I used to set out his coffee cup and a spoon every night, grind the coffee beans, and load the machine so he'd only have to push a button. Just push one button."

Bunny looks at me with tenderness. Her fists clench on the table.

"I was a good wife," I repeat. Tears are shooting from my eyes like ineffectual bullets. "I have to go now."

"Would you like me to take A this weekend?" Bunny asks, without a hint of inference in her voice.

"I guess so. Yes," I say, leaning forward from the waist cantilevered as I stand, like someone with fused vertebrae. My face is barely contained and may fly apart. I walk out of the house, closing the door gently behind me.

Oh, no. Oh, no, I am whispering to myself as I walk briskly to my car, holding one sleeve of my sweatshirt to my face like a tourniquet. I partially run, get inside the car quickly, and lock all the doors. I stretch out across the backseat and keen into the enclosed space.

I think about the cocktail napkin. I think of the feminine inscription on the book of Zen Poetry that I had almost managed to forget. I almost had it erased.

xo

Me

The Adrenaline Spin,
the Blue-Face Event

At our former nuptial home there were many events. Such as The Day I Threw The Lamp. (One needn't describe; it's self-explanatory—suffice it to say we had two gaily painted rooster lamps in the living room, and now there is only one.) Then there was The Day N Kicked The Barstool and it careened across the cherrywood dining room table. There's a skid mark, I can see it right now, can slide a nickel into it, so deep is it. The nickel stands up.

When it happened, this little foray into domestic violence, my main feeling was hate and relief. Hate the man who would kick a barstool, his face turning almost blue with rage, and relief that the new dining room table finally had its first genuine scratch.

N complained of his unhappiness whereas I bore mine like a Brownie badge. I like to think I acted out less than he did, but I am probably wrong. I can't see anymore.

At the end, I could almost hear the audible *snap* as he would go Tasmanian devil on me—if I asked him too many questions, or if A had a tantrum after N was home after a long day. His eyes would bulge and he became hideous to behold, a ghoul, deftly sweeping out of the house.

What did I do? I bought nonfiction books. The literature.

Men Are from Mars, Women Are from Venus
Relationship Rescue
How to Get What You Want and Want What You Have
The Seat of the Soul
The Good Marriage
The Sexual Self
The Seven Principles for Making Marriage Work
Sacred Contracts
Mars and Venus Starting Over
Getting the Love You Want
Spiritual Divorce

They make a long, solid row on the bookshelf. I haven't yet read any, but I plan to as soon as I can properly focus.

The Papers

It was a Tuesday when N's lawyer, Joseph Spikenard, had the papers served, somewhere between two and three in the afternoon. I heard the doorbell ring with finality and resonance that had seemed previously absent; it seemed to ring and ring. I opened the door not to find a tall man in an executioner's hood as I had envisioned, but a small brown-haired woman.

"Are you Suzanne Finnamore?"

"Yes, I am," I murmur.

I seem to have momentarily left my body: I have won something unexpectedly. Bunny drifts out on the porch in round sunglasses, carrying a paring knife and a lime.

I am handed a thick white legal-size envelope with my name handwritten on it. I know that inside this envelope there is not a coupon for a free salad with a large pizza, or an invitation to a fund-raiser for Guatemala. The roses in the front yard have misunderstood; have chosen this very day to begin to bloom, a vast pinkness in the periphery of my vision.

"Can I sign this and just give it back to you now?" I ask.

"No," the woman says. She takes a step backwards. As though I could stain her. "You have to read it before you sign," she explains gently.

Then, incredibly, I say to this woman, "Thank you."

Bunny looks at me blankly, as though nonplussed. She tugs at her earring before she tosses a few words over my head to the woman's back.

"Yes. THANK YOU. And say hello to Judas Iscariot."

She does not turn around, the petition server, but she does have a spring in her step as she crosses the quiet street, climbs into her Mercedes C-Class sedan, and drives away.

I drop my head onto my chest. It is so heavy. I scan the papers in my hands and see N's signature at the bottom of the first page; I hand it to Bunny, cover my face. The javelin twists.

Bunny says, "I am so sorry. I would do anything to fix this for you. Anything."

She walks around the room, paring the zest from the lime for cocktail hour, which like CNN is round the clock.

"Would you like me to kill him? Right now I think I could. With these hands."

Bunny holds up her two hands, festooned with cocktail rings.

I go downstairs to put the divorce petition away in N's night-stand drawer. I fantasize very briefly that there is a gun inside the drawer, but there is none. He has thoughtfully cleaned out this drawer. I stare at the empty drawer, a kind of coffin. I slide the drawer shut and throw the papers under the bed.

I am afraid of the divorce papers, particularly the unassail-able and undeniable image of N's familiar signature at the bot-tom. I feel N is signing away A and me. There is that, and there is also the Irreconcilable Differences line. It seems so catchall, so vague. You could say that about anyone, any man and woman at all. Jesus and Mary Magdalene: "Irreconcilable Differences." JFK and Jackie, anyone at all. It's built into the man-woman thing. What kind of paltry reason is that? "Insanity" is another box to be checked on the divorce petition, the only alternative to "Irreconcilable Differences." I would like to check it.

If only he could die. I know this is not a Christian thought, and that if in fact he were to die, I would mourn him for years, and would also have to promote him to tarnished saint: another travesty. Time refuses to slow down or move backwards; I want to say *Stop,* but I have no voice in this. He has in essence cut my cords, in this one vital important instance.

Upstairs I can hear my mother quietly talking on the

telephone to my stepfather, their end-of-day bread-and-butter call. I feel a wave of envy that pushes the air from my lungs. I climb into A's daybed. I have A. That, I reason, is a great deal to have in one's life. Maybe you only get one person to fully love who will love you back, and A is mine. I feel his warm mammalian feet against my stomach, tethering me to earth, soothing me and also reminding me of my responsibilities in the here and now.

I must fully use my eyes. They are swollen, rinsed, and freshened, can take in more. *Wonderful.*

It's the beginning of seeing what is actually happening: My marriage and family is breaking apart. I resolve to miss nothing of importance.

Sublet

It wasn't that long ago that N was stroking and kissing the insides of my thighs, whispering about what he considered my two magnificent legs. He wondered aloud how he could ever let a woman with legs this good go.

"You'd be a fool," I'd offered. "A narcissistic, moral degenerate . . . ?"

Silence except for the kissing sounds. Several months too late I realize this was not a hypothetical question. This was very bad, but his kisses were very good. He was expert at layering smooth caresses with memorably eloquent compliments. He had an abundance of presence and outstanding technique.

"Are you sure you want to remember this?" Lisa says, listening to me reminisce on the phone this morning as I clean out N's coat closet. I throw his coats onto the ground, the dead coats. I will donate them to the Cerebral Palsy Society.

"Remember what?" I mumble.

Lisa says, "Suzanne. Remember the divorce petition? It was hand-delivered."

"Yes. Well. He's like a dog with a bone," I say. "He needs his Happiness era. Of course, he'll be miserable."

"Oh, yes," Lisa says. "That."

I tell Lisa about N's new sublet in Russian Hill. To me, the fact that he has not bought property indicates huge ambivalence. I used to loathe ambivalence, now I adore it. Ambivalence is my new best friend.

"Sublet," Lisa repeats dryly, as though she is reading items off a convict's rap sheet. "Russian Hill."

"It's interesting how he has a problem with change," I observe. I am drinking the last of the Chardonnay straight from the bottle as I open a Chilean Merlot.

Emotionally, it is an environmental disaster; I feel certain that it cannot get any worse.

This is another error on my part. Because at the very next full moon, A tells me that he and Daddy and a Woman went to the zoo.

Who?

"*Who* went to the zoo with you and Daddy?" I ask.

"A Woman," A says.

"Is the Woman a pretty girl?" I ask, though I know the answer, knew it the moment she was first uttered. A nods solemnly.

"Oh. Okay. Great!" I say, and hear my heart beating, racing ahead to meet its enemy. Woman, I think. Okay. Some fucking Thing Woman. Now I know. Thing Woman and A and N at the zoo. Replacement complete. The End. *Fin*. And without thinking better of it, I picture the entire scene. People would think they were the real family. A not knowing he is part of a lie.

"Xo Me" is from Thing Woman, I think as my head caves in. Involuntarily I see the scene in *You Only Live Twice* where James Bond is almost killed by a slim sexy black reed dripping with thick poison, a wet frond that nefariously distends from the ceiling of his thatched Japanese luxury condominium. He wakes up, a roll to the side, and his real girlfriend gets it in the kisser. It's so evil. So Thing Woman.

I call N and say two words: *I know*.

He tries to respond, but I hang up the phone. Take it off the hook. Scream into my bed pillow until I can't talk. Cry. Scream. Come out of my room, prepare macaroni and cheese for A, watch television with A, kiss A good night.

Cry. Scream. Cry. Scream.

Bond Girl

I reenact the James Bond movie scene for Bunny, over pizza at Round Table.

"Thing Woman. It's not a real name," I croak to Bunny. *Après* screaming I still can't talk clearly, which comes in handy since I plan to never speak to N again, or at least in the foreseeable future.

"She's not a real person," Bunny says with conviction, stirring her chai and then tapping the spoon loudly against the side of the glass before she puts it down.

However, Thing Woman is undoubtedly real and has stepped in and neatly filled my role. We construct her in our minds.

"Just like the ingenue in *All About Eve*, Thing Woman is always ready to step in," I intone.

"No, she's not that ambitious. But she is ruthless, and probably a knockout. Don't kid yourself." Bunny throws the words out as if they are immaterial.

"Oh. I'm sorry, I assumed she was grotesque, Mom. Are you kidding me? I'd *kill* to be able to kid myself," I say. "I may still kill. It's not over yet."

"There may be many good reasons to kill her now . . . ," Bunny says, gesturing for the grated cheese.

"Thing Woman secretly thinks she could be a Bond girl," I say. "Invincible."

"Yesss . . . a Bond girl . . . if she weren't such a genius . . . ,"
Bunny muses.

"Mother of God," I say, touching my forehead down to the
table. I stand and walk toward my mother's LeBaron and she
follows me, throwing down a tip as she goes.

Signs

In the end of our marriage, N and I went to Hawaii. We think
Hawaii is a good idea because we feel it will be easy with the new
baby, A, in Hawaii. We plan to snorkel, despite the tide. The tide
is stronger than we know.

I am snorkeling without fins. I have skinny legs and large, flat
feet; I find fins gratuitous. I fear looking foolish, something a
thirty-nine-year-old mother shambling backwards into the tide
with large rubber fins cannot avoid. I'm tracking the schools of
angelfish and the Picasso triggerfish, shadowing the gelatinous
eels that exploit surface, the eels that one doesn't see without
looking up. Their eyes are steel bolts in blue transparency, their
organs oddly visible. I revel in the selfishness of the sport, the iso-
lation, the unapologetic nature of the sea, how it welcomes without interview. Water with its innate relief and the attendant fear
that we will not be able to return to the dry world. That we may

not want to. The sea from whence we came, as JFK said. All the best people are dead, I think.

I swim idly, breathing through my mouth. The sea urchins, the angelfish, the white spotted grouper all hold my fascination, but it is the exquisite ornate wrasse that drove me to pursuit, that beckoned me to the deep water. There are fewer of them, the ornate wrasse. Did their splendor make them exclusive? Or was it their neon colors, hues unnatural, gaudy, and false? This also drew me, the falseness. In so many senseless deaths, beauty is to blame.

At one point I looked back at the shore and saw that it was far, but not out of range; I could easily make it back. I pressed my face down into the sea again, nestled close to my own heartbeat, watching the sun negotiate the island clouds and brighten the water with sudden fleeting warmth. When the warm pockets came I would stop kicking, float. Though it was deep here, nothing was quite as it seemed. Reefs could rise up suddenly massive and slice one's knees. I was artful, careful, had been cut before. I moved aquiline, weightless, and free.

People who couldn't swim seemed sad to me. I have always swum, do not remember learning. I was born knowing, but of course that couldn't be true. At some point I learned. It's frequently the good swimmers who drown.

A liked the water but frowned at the waves, the sound of them. He had cried when I held him at the water's edge, when I ventured out slightly and a wave came and knocked us both to our knees. Soaked, A screamed and arched his back wildly, just six months old. I felt someone would walk calmly from the up-per beach to take A away, to safety, away from me; I didn't feel truly qualified as a mother yet. As a swimmer, I felt qualified.

I still thought this when I realized I could see the top of the ocean, the whitecaps collecting and dissolving. I saw I had drifted too deep into the ocean, but I still believed I could get back. I hadn't taken into account the tide, which was strong enough to thwart swimmers but not strong enough to be called a riptide. There had been a large sign on the beach: ALL WAVES ARE DAN-GEROUS. I'd read the sign and gone on.

I swam hard toward shore, heart thrumming. I felt it was a race, a test. I had always enjoyed tests, had always believed I could do well without studying. But the shore did not grow closer. The tide pushed me back to the ocean. *What is this?* I thought. My left leg cramped. I decided to rest for a moment and wait for the cramp to pass; I decided to stop and rest. How heavy life is, the trying part, until it stops, I thought. At the same time, I realized that if I rested here, I might drown.

Fins are necessary, quite lovely things.

I swam harder despite the cramp, zigzagging against the waves. I never considered the real danger of drowning.

I make it back. I have a child; I have to make it back. My luck held.

All my life, I should not have worried so much about looking foolish; I see that now. Signs matter. And all waves are danger-ous, especially the ones you refuse to see coming.

II
Anger

*Better to hate than to grieve. I sing in praise
of hate, and all its attendant energy.
I sing a hymn to the death of love.*

—Fay Weldon

Knives

I sharpen knives at the sink. The hard sound of the long iron steel renewing an edge, honing my blades into something other than dull, is satisfying. I think of my silence, too, as a golden ax that can be sharpened slowly over time and held just at the wayside.

An unraveling red kimono is tightly bound against my nakedness, my feet bare, my long hair spread out. My breasts move freely as I attend to the large bread knife with majestic, firm sweeps, alternating sides to make it evenly sharp, its threat a regular one; next the long carving knife. Because I have to do something, don't I. If I just sit and woolgather, I begin to think about interesting projects, like smashing tibias.

I have not spoken to my soon-to-be-ex husband, N, in days. I am not thinking about the future.

Carefully, I wipe the knife clean with a soft cloth. I review what I know once again, confronting the monolith now alien and almost unconnected to me: my marriage.

Five years long, I know that. Beginning with pleasurable and regular sex, the communion of books and food and childbirth and mutual preference swaying high and sweet and then, more and more, its simple lack. An absence opened from N's side of the marriage, a different tone of silence.

As marital deformities go, ours were sufficiently small so as not to be an obstruction, sufficiently large so as not to go unnoticed. From a distance it looked like a good marriage. I had almost convinced myself it was like that up close. I thought it was normal. I rationalized that I would never have married a man too encompassing, no challenge there: no friction. I adored him more, added sentiment and romance from my side to even things out, poured love into baby A and wished for the best.

Sometime during the seasons and the years and the arguments about money and sexual positions and diapers, it became punitive, the silence. It became a void; a place I could add to and see no difference, and I had seen that and I had blinked. I had blinked and that, I see now, was the beginning of my own undoing. Because I decided that what a good wife and a new mother would do would be to correct her own faults, and simply expand to fill the space.

At this point in time it shocks me, literally sends a raw jangling nerve through my body, how wrong a person can be, to call it "Fighting for Love." Call it "Keeping the Family Together." I mentally issue myself a dunce cap, tall and pointy.

I see N drifting farther on and becoming a speck. Instead of becoming more people, the prime objective of family life, we had become fewer. A was magnificent, with silk skin and pearl teeth, and he made no real difference, he too was nothing against the void, a secret place for N to retire and withdraw and count his emotional change. Places for N to go without his actually moving house. And someone else had taken in what he had withdrawn. A woman. A Thing Woman. Had sucked it right on in.

Now N had two *I Dream of Jeannie* women in his magic lamp, with just him in the cockpit as Major Nelson, the authority figure who gets to choose his new Jeannie. It must have been a challenging decision for him, to choose contestant A or contestant B. One contestant came with a wiggly baby boy, mitigating the choice with an extra variable.

Knowing N's superb taste, I ascertained that Thing Woman would be practically flawless, more tolerant, better educated, more attractive, and with a lower BMI score. I was sure she spoke several more languages and went to a better university. I know my sex . . . when pressed, we work the odds and numbers before we commit to a serious bet; preparation and research on the opponent's flaws is everything. This wasn't difficult, as during their liaisons and e-mails and phone calls, I imagine N gently yet methodically detailed my shortcomings, and a sentient woman would take care to avoid my personal faults and bad behavior when it came to designing, finessing, and executing her own coup. In the end the right Jeannie was crystal clear and he went in for the slow and civilized kill.

As eventual as autumnal rain, soon N would not talk about anything involving feelings, his whereabouts or actions, or my needs. He began to fly into a perfect rage and leave the house for extended periods of time. I now see his initial strategy: I would toss him out; he would be absolved of guilt. Instead, I just became depressed. N insisted there was no other woman in his life; when

I asked questions he compared me to the CIA, his face twisted in disgust. Clearly I was crazy and paranoid as well, and soon I was on antidepressants. Perhaps the worst crime: letting a spouse believe they've lost their mind, and bundling them off to a psychiatrist rather than being honest. Still, I am very glad for this now. It would be a shame to be incapacitated at such a time as this.

I pick up a paring knife from Chicago Cutlery. Throw it up in the air, catch it.

I wonder exactly when it was that my marriage ended. I believe it is possible to pinpoint, and that knowing will release me. With the right cocktail of wine and nicotine, I can almost believe marriage is not an indelible part of my life. Although N wishes it so, it might not disappear without a bit of trouble. My trouble and N's and I suppose even his girlfriend, Madam X.

I am afraid I am going to be of some trouble.

I resolve not to ask A about where he has been with his daddy on their biweekly visits. If, perhaps, A can remember a strange woman hanging on Daddy's arm? Does A know anything about this woman? Anything at all? Does he think he can bring Mommy this person's wallet?

A is highly keen, could shed light on dim corners, but there will be no pawns in this game. There will be only Queens and Kings, and perhaps a Rook. Yes, that's how I think of Thing Woman. A Rook.

I feel real regret; I would like to ask A several hundred questions, evenly spaced over a lifetime. Instead I must begin the discovery process without A, must in fact shield him from any and all sorts of harm or unfiltered truth.

I stroke the knife away from myself at a thirty-degree angle, the blade and the steel forming an initial X at the base.

Can I settle this without knowing the details of my own ignorance, the secrets generously studded throughout my life with N, or do I require more details? Of course I do, I absolutely require more details, some piecemeal version of the truth. I am human, a detriment to the smooth, successful completion of divorce.

In the meantime, I've been squirreling away my own earnings, needing to know that the worst could happen and I would survive. Survival being key to revenge.

Someday I will have revenge. I know in advance to keep this to myself, and everyone will be happier. I do understand that I am expected to forgive N and his girlfriend in a timely fashion, and move on to a life of vegetarian cooking and difficult yoga positions and self-realization, and make this so much easier and more pleasant for all concerned. Just move right along and go quietly: A and I, hand in hand, forgetting there was a time when we were all a family. Doing it for our own good. Doing it for everyone, really.

This, I glean, is what N and Thing Woman theorized and subsequently did. Their life seems to go on swimmingly within their bubble; they likely feel that divorce is for everyone's benefit and they project that confidence into the world. This much I know from the sly undercurrent of gossip that one or two well-intentioned acquaintances can't seem to leave out of their sparse Breaking News calls: My unwanted militia of suburban spies report that the new couple is serene. They eat fine cuisine and walk through Russian Hill holding hands as they gaze into the boutiques and jewelry shops. They are both impeccably dressed; they are pleased and unabashed and bold. They feel life is for the taking, and that everyone deserves happiness no matter what the cost. I must remember these tricks if I ever decide to have my soul surgically removed.

I move on to the chopping knives.

A Bad Day

Bad day today. Blue Cross called to say N is kicking me off his medical policy. A, they think, is still on N's policy. It's not clear at this point.

I think about renting a chain saw and sawing off the top of my head, the part that Emily Dickinson says is taken off when one reads great poetry. Also I think about stabbing myself with my letter opener; I toy with the tip against my sternum. I know there are enough pills in the house to put an end to consciousness. Between the sedatives and the sleeping pills and back medicine, I am a veritable KevorkianMobile. I imagine just such a cart, loaded with mega-dose sedatives and with a music box that plays like an ice-cream truck, tinkly music, maybe "Love Is a Many-Splendored Thing"—the ice-cream man who is really the impromptu suicide man. I visualize abandoned women running out from their ranch-style homes in fuzzy slippers to catch the truck before it passes their street. Running out in chenille bathrobes, what Lisa calls "The Uniform of the Distraught."

I know I can't do anything drastic because of A, and even without A, I'm sure I wouldn't. I am 99 percent sure.

N has not called in three days, and even though it is easier not to speak with him, it reinforces the distance that is going to be the mainstay of our what? Relationship? Surely it's not a friendship, although I admire those who can form instant friendly bonds with their estranged spouses; I imagine that they have not had the passion that eventually blots out all civility. I'm happy for other people who are doing their divorces right, and who were never meant for each other.

The Grief Counselor

Nadine Blackman, PhD. When I look across the room at her straight white pageboy and her pacific eyes, the irises like two slivers of quartz, I inwardly groan. Nadine oozes serenity, almost bliss. It is very difficult to be around someone like this while I am mired in my own highly personal and unique hammered shit phase of recovery.

Nadine's husband died of a coronary, ten years ago. It is her job to de-grief me. Yet in her neat black suit and pumps, and despite the modern furniture and the Noguchi lamp that floats like a white head beside her chair, Nadine manages somehow to look pleased and interested, as though she is tuning in to an episode of a favorite forensic drama. Imagine if the television spit out a hundred-dollar bill during the commercial break: This is Nadine's world.

"How can I fully grieve what is still in motion?" I ask her. "Shoes are still dropping all over the place. I'm not kidding," I say. "It's Normandy out there."

Nadine raises her eyebrows, for what? Surely she is not surprised, not here. This is the pyramid of denial, the teepee of the split.

"But it *is* happening, Suzanne," Nadine says. "The divorce is in play."

"It's surreal," I continue. "I still see him constantly. I get checks, too. I never got checks before. Also, I feel forced. It feels like I am being asked to manufacture some very profound, final grief and hand it over."

Nadine claps her hands together once and says, "Forget grief. What do you feel inside right now?"

"I've never felt crazier than I do now, or more flat; more deflated of desires and expectations."

"What else?"

"I feel furious. I feel erased . . . mired in hardening cement and rejected and shamed."

"YOU feel shamed?"

"Hell yes."

Nadine waits, her eyes widening and off-focus, as she seems to check with the spirit world for input.

I describe some of my dreams. I reveal last night's dream where we're at Morton's, and I stab N in the thigh with a steak knife while he is perusing the raw meat cart, smirking. He was smirking at the meat.

At this point, Nadine theorizes that this stabbing dream is more grounded and real, as opposed to my recurring, rather pleasant dreams wherein I am flying, or walking a foot aboveground.

"You want to rise above this situation, to not experience it," she says, pointing one square taupe fingernail at me.

"I don't see any benefit to experiencing this portion of my life," I say.

"I see," Nadine says. She smiles, like a dolphin. Just the corners of her mouth, but with her jaw slightly open.

"It's not denial," I assert. "It's not as if I expect things to dramatically improve. In fact I quite clearly envision them getting exponentially worse. I'm going slowly yet surely into deeper and deeper debt and will die alone, a cliché.

"In fact," I say, stretching my legs out straight into the room, "it's already happening. In a nutshell? I'm fucked."

Nadine then stands up to deliver her assessment as she adjusts the temperature gauge on the wall. As she squints at its dial, she announces that I have this very negative voice inside me; it says things like, *You're no good,* and *It will never work.*

Nadine says she thinks it is a man. She spins around to face the couch as she says it, putting her hands on her hips.

"The Sawed-Off Madman," I say dryly. I recognize him right away. Privately, I thought everyone had one, like a pituitary gland.

"I would guess that fifty percent of it is your ex husband," Nadine says.

It seems a very specific bid: I'll take Famous Authors for five hundred. I cross my legs and try to think of actual instances during our marriage where N was critical, and arrive at only one or two, but also a vague sense of unease, as though if I kept going I would be hobbled.

"Now that we've flushed this voice out," Nadine says, "you should really look at what he's *saying*. . . ." Nadine seems horrified by the Sawed-Off Madman.

I tell her what he's saying.

The Sawed-Off Madman drones on about my modest success and how it's all been an accident, minimizing every reached goal as though it were something a chimpanzee would find tedious. He sees my marriage as an unmitigated catastrophe, a flaming zeppelin. He knows I am to blame for a great deal of everything that is wrong, if not every single thing that is wrong. And not just here, everywhere. Worldwide wrong.

I tell Nadine this, who touches her chin, like a don. She muses, rocking slightly in her red Eames chair. Then she says that the Sawed-Off Madman is someone we may need to get rid of.

I agree. At the same time I am acutely aware of the Sawed-Off Madman in the back of the room with his arms folded, saying:

What does she know? She's your grief counselor; she's getting paid to say those things. Where did she go to school? And her husband's dead. She has it fucking made.

Return of Françoise

My mother-in-law, Françoise, weaves in and out of my life, somehow managing to call just as I am wishing to speak to anyone, anyone at all. I see her area code on my phone and I brace myself, light a cigarette, and pick up.

"Hello, Françoise. *Bonsoir*."

"Suzanne!?" she shouts. She is eighty years old and somewhat hard of hearing. Françoise has the thickest Parisian accent I have ever heard from an American, although she has lived in Chicago since 1945. She is a very good woman and she always speaks her mind. This is bearable only because she is not my mother, she is N's mother.

"Ah! *Bonsoir. En bien ou en mal,* Suzanne?" she asks.

"I am shitty, Françoise," I say. "I miss your son and there is something very wrong with your son to have left his family. He's fucked up."

"I cannot 'ear this, Suzanne! Imagine if someone were saying this about your son. I am iz mozzer," she says.

"Yes. I know," I reply. I sigh. "And I don't blame you."

Naturally, I do blame Françoise. I blame her for having N in the first place. She was young, she was beautiful, she was married to a doctor, and she was intelligent. She could have abstained from producing her first son. It was wrong on a variety of levels. I am a little tense, I realize. It's probably Françoise's fault for calling at this time. Although I notice there is never a truly good time to have a nice long chat with one's mother-in-law, unless you are having an extraordinary life and marriage and your mother-in-law is, say, Maureen Dowd, or Indira Gandhi. Someone of that ilk.

"I'm glad you don' blame me," Françoise says. "I feel sad."

"Très, très triste . . . ," I say.

I don't speak French, but Françoise brings out the imposter in me. I can speak a kind of pidgin French to Françoise, and she allows it. She is actually a good mother-in-law, sending A the most wonderful clothes from Lord & Taylor in Chicago, and always including a small gift for me. A piece of tasteful jewelry, some Coco Chanel body cream. Françoise is fine. It's her son who is menacing the earth.

"When you go out, always wear makeup," Françoise advises. We've come to that portion of the show.

"Yes?" I ask.

Makeup? Isn't that how this whole travesty of justice began? Yet she has a terrible tendency to be right about matters of love and food and fashion—as maddening as the French are about these matters, they generally have quite solid, politically incorrect advice.

"Always. And dress nicely. You never know," Françoise croons.

"No, you never do know," I agree with Françoise. Although I am not contemplating meeting my next husband in line at the market, or discovering true love as I ride a cable car in San Francisco. I am contemplating heart attacks and strokes and electric wires that dance crazily on city streets, Russian Hill in particular.

Gypsy Curse

I curse N in the garage. I gypsy curse him.

Until you do right by me, everything you do will go wrong. You will have no happiness. You gave me a ring and a baby, but then you leave. It's not enough. It's not fucking enough, I shout, wondering from which film this scene is; it feels very familiar.

N is loading boxes into his truck. I've painstakingly separated his photographs from mine; I toss his big black tied-off bags of photos at him like an angry elf. Then I furiously rake pine needles from the walkway. It feels terrible. After he is gone I stumble into the house and throw myself onto the couch. I babble incoherently on the phone to Bunny. She listens gently; I know that in her mind she is thrusting chunky bamboo shoots under N's nails.

Things are not going well. I feel incendiary, a wildfire. My spirit licks at the gates of a very elaborate, customized, and distracting emotional Hades.

The very next day, while changing an audiotape of *The Four Agreements*, I ram my car into a neighborhood giant redwood tree. The six-hundred-year-old tree meets the 1997 four-door sedan. It lets the car receive the correction. I can still see over the top of the buckled hood, and I take this as a sign to hang a U-turn and drive home at once.

I gun the engine and careen back up my hill as a strange

neighbor runs after my car, waving his arms. When the tow truck arrives, they find that I've broken the axle, and the front wheels are sideways. It hurts my eyes to look at the mangled bumper, hanging by what appears to be a series of rubber bands.

"Gotta watch those curses," Bunny observes.

Dodge Ram

Ron is bringing over his 1980 Dodge Ram four-wheel-drive tonnage truck. It is a large white truck with a bench seat covered with a horse blanket, a stick shift, and two big side rear mirrors supported by four iron spikes. I can see all around me now. It is a plain truck but good in an emergency; it seems that I am in a near constant state of emergency.

"Take the Ram," Ron says, and he is practically weeping as he hands over the keys, he loves it so much.

He looks down at his work boots and then straight at me.

"I'd like to drive it up his ass," Ron says.

I gasp and feel happy all over. Just the desire to defend us is enough, just the idea of it.

Medieval Acts: How Animosity Starts

Today N calls to decree that I can't move to Tesuque, New Mexico, as I may in fact want to. Because of A and the presence of N's lawyer, Joseph Spikenard, who I am sure knows the very letter of the law right down to the last greasy syllable, I can't move beyond the county line. It is as though I am a prime suspect for a major crime. The fact that N walked out on us is meaningless; I stand accused, a resident of the state of California, where the rights of fathers are strictly protected. Fathers and serial killers. I mentally note that Charles Manson is still alive just a few miles away at San Quentin, that he has a Web site.

I call my mother and my accountant, in that order.

You have to buy him out of the house, they say.

I have to worry about money again. Not fretting about money has been a terrific stress reducer since marriage, but it's over. The ride is over, step out of the boat, ma'am.

Therefore, I told N he couldn't pick up A this afternoon, because I was absolutely sure that if I saw him, I would spit in his face.

He said, "You can't keep me from seeing my son."

"Right, yes," I said. "But can you accept the face-spitting part?"

The snag about marriage is, it isn't worth the divorce. My new doctrine is, never marry. I won't ever again. It is absolute swill. It's not just my marriage. It's all marriages except a handful. Marriage is a conspiracy from Tiffany's, florists, the diamond industry, and Christian fundamentalists. The only thing good about it is the diamond ring, the wedding gifts, and the honeymoon. A, I could have gotten anywhere. I could have gotten A from a turkey baster and a lovely gay man with a college education and a pleasant disposition. *IF ONLY I'D HAD THAT MUCH SENSE AT THE TIME.* I'm sending turkey basters to all my single girlfriends, with holly tassels, for Christmas.

It's fairly simple, my state of mind: I want N dead. It comes on suddenly, a meteor of repressed anger. I want his mother dead too, perhaps his whole extended family and his friends as well. They should all go. And I am ashamed of these thoughts and the fact that I married him, and I'm vaguely disgusted that he is A's father. I feel horrified by it, physically repulsed. A terrible mistake has been made, one with miraculously good results: our son.

Someday I hope I can stop hating A's father, but right now I do. He has betrayed and abandoned me, and there is nothing for it. I have to look it full in the face and say, *It is over. I was left* and *it's over.* Two very hard truths to swallow, but both at once? Ghastly. I can see why my mind has taken this long to process it; my brain was waiting for me to be strong enough to bear it, and I can. I can bear it. I'm not going to die. That's another thing I was wrong about. I am far too angry to die.

The third truth is that he is my child's father, and that is not going away. Unless he dies. So I hope he dies, I hope it with all my mashed heart. Conversely, it also wants instant peace. It wants to not look upon his face ever again or hear his voice. . . .

I feel it deserves this release. I can't even enjoy wishing him dead, because he is A's father and A loves him. No, A adores him, as I adored him at the beginning, only with much more élan and confidence.

Bad Smoker

I don't want N dead. He came over and was upset that he'd lost his wallet, so I had to hug him and that of course made me not want him dead anymore.

"I hate this," I say to Bunny on the telephone while I smoke in A's tree house. "Can I just please have one consistent feeling about this person? That I could live with."

"You'd be the first," Bunny says.

In time, I will be much less dependent on cigarettes and alcohol. Much, much less dependent. More self-contained; a kind of Amazonian queen mother with shearling boots is what I will be. But right now I am a bad smoker.

The moment A is asleep, I creep to my attic room, fling open the small glass door, and smoke like a fiend, like a chimney, like the little engine that couldn't. I am a terrible smoker, dripping ashes everywhere and losing the head of the cigarette in my hair. I set fire to not one, not two, but five chenille throws. One mattress pad went down while I was on the phone to New York, as did two pillows and a luxury comforter.

I smoke in odd places that aren't in front of A. I smoke inside the garage and on top of our roof and behind the woodpile and outside on the tiny balcony, for A's sake. It would be sad and wrong in so many ways to self-combust at this time. I set a mitten on fire while lighting a cigarette. Yet I feel I am safe on the balcony. There are succulents here, and concrete won't burn, and stars seem to leer down at me and say, *See everything. Miss nothing.*

Shoot the Moon

N and I have a fight scene straight out of *Shoot the Moon*, with Diane Keaton and Albert Finney. It ends with N running over my foot very slightly with his SUV, just the side of my shoe and not my actual foot. A is watching it all like a Keane painting. Afterward A seems fine but I know he will turn out to be an angry street person due to this. We didn't yell, N and I, we muttered with great vehemence and urgency. He called me a harpy; I was hanging on to his car as he drove away. I remember thinking how probable it was that the car was going to win, but I was willing to try based on sheer principle. I didn't want to be the first to let go.

That very afternoon, A and I attend a birthday party for a three-year-old, Ryan. Everyone from A's day care center is there, all the mommies and daddies and children, the whole gorgeous clan.

"How is your heart?" asks Darlene, mother of Sonia, who is technically A's girlfriend.

Unhesitant, I say, "It's shattered. Thank you for asking."

A woman with tricolor false eyelashes is twisting balloons into animals and hats; swords for the boys, magic fairy wands for the girls.

We talk. Darlene worries aloud that her husband works with a lot of attractive young women; she herself is forty. I tell her it's not about age. "Little thing called character," I say, thinking, *Accepting marital advice from me: the height of lunacy.*

We both nod meaningfully and gaze around the party, drinking tepid mineral water. Couples, couples, couples, most of them with bigger families, new fatter babies. Somewhere a balloon breaks. The crying begins, and the hushing and the carrying off of the young.

How to Tell a Liar

1. A change in the voice's pitch.
2. A change in the rate of speech.
3. A sudden increase in the number of "ums" and "ahs."
4. A change in eye contact. Normally, one makes eye contact

one-quarter to one-half of the time. If suddenly, at the convenient moment to lie, he's staring at you or looking away, beware.

5. A turning of one's body away from you, even if just slightly.

6. Suddenly being able to see the white on the top and bottom of a person's eyes, not just the sides.

7. A hand reaching, even if momentarily, to cover part of the face, especially the mouth.

8. Nervous movement of the feet or legs.

Of course, in order to notice a change, you need a baseline. So you must first watch the person when talking about innocuous issues.

Also look for mixed signals. When someone's telling the truth, her words, her face, and her body language is all congruent. For example, if a person is honestly saying that she likes you, her face is usually relaxed, offering a gentle smile and warm eyes. Her body is calm and open. But when she's lying, something is usually inconsistent. In the most obvious case, she may be saying she likes you, but she's not smiling. She may even have a clenched fist. Better liars can muster a smile, but it doesn't look natural. Even better liars can put on a convincing smile, but their eyes aren't smiling. Still better liars can control their entire face, but their bodies seem closed or cold. Look for mismatches between words and body language.

When you've gotten a signal—a change in body language or a mixed signal that the person may be lying—ask for more information about the same topic. Are those same lying signs apparent? That can confirm your suspicions.

Of course, there's no foolproof way to detect lying. Some people are terrific at covering themselves up, especially if they are naturally emotionally flat or have practiced their lying skills over many years—certain political leaders come to mind. But if you look for behavior changes and mixed signals at lying-expedient moments, you will improve your lie detector.

Bereavement Overload

Nadine says I'm in Bereavement Overload.

"We need to identify the primary loss and the secondary losses . . . e.g., loss of status. Going from wife to divorcée, single mother. Being betrayed, which is the epoxy of all the worst grief," Nadine says.

Techniques to relieve grief include:

List making
Crafts
Naps
Talking to clergy
Journaling
Altar creation

Flowers
Rocking
Wailing
Sighing
Screaming
Voice dialogues
Animal sounds
Gibberish
Crawling
Yoga
Aerobics classes
Nostril breathing (Take right thumb and press left nostril
shut. Breathe.)
Mouth breathing
Essential oils
Gingerroot
Tansy
Lavender
Grapefruit
Lemongrass (three drops)
Ylang-ylang
Melaleuca

Snakes

Christian and I grew up together, although we are by no means adults, especially when we're combined. We bring out the very worst tendencies in each other, and this is very gratifying. I need a friend to be evil with, one I can edge as close to the edge as I want to. It's like having a second trapeze artist, if one likes the trapeze.

After college, we used to write television and radio jingles together for a small music house. Christian stopped writing jingles and eventually became a network television studio executive. I went on to write meaningful poems of personal growth. Then I got a job proofreading, and after a goodly time I was an account coordinator and finally an advertising copywriter, at which point jingles entered my life in a terribly real way.

Christian has no children, one ex wife, and a yacht, which broke his heart when it ran aground in Catalina.

I force Christian to visit for the weekend, telling him it is what Gandhi would do. I was glib on the phone, but by my very request he knew I was in trouble. He flew his toy plane up. Christian shaves his tanned head every morning, is as rich as Croesus, perpetually optimistic, and genuinely interested in A. I don't know how he got where he is, but I suspect it is sheer chemistry and a terrifying honesty. He has had his pilot's license since he was eighteen, although he looks exactly like someone who would accidentally crash a plane into a mountain while telling a joke. He picks me up in his rental car. We hug extensively.

"Writing anything?" Christian asks, briskly rubbing his palms together.

"Some," I reply. "Mostly suicide notes."

Christian doesn't laugh. Instead he takes both my ears tenderly in his hands, pulls me close to his face, and says, "I think you're great." Then he peels off toward town.

"Actually?" I say to Christian, stretching my bare arm out the window to feel the wind. "I've thought about suicide but lack the energy. Also there is the problem of the note. I would end up coming across as banal."

Christian nods knowingly. To him, my marriage is like a show that has been canceled. I get the sense he has more interesting projects to discuss but is making an effort to Talk About Feelings.

I glance ahead and realize that he has veered his rented Lincoln onto the wrong road, in the opposite direction of Kentucky Fried Chicken, where we are going to drive through and procure grease.

"DELAY OF CHICKEN!" I shout, pointing to the correct road.

He does a 180. We laugh like teenagers. Minutes later we leave the premises laden with the Family Pack: twenty pieces, plus mashed potatoes, gravy, and coleslaw. We both like Original Recipe; this seems to me a good basis for my second marriage, to Christian, but he has a new girlfriend. She has a classy name and is lovely and kind, as are presumably all the women in Venice Beach, California. It's like he lives in this really great box.

How good it feels to be with Christian. To laugh out loud and mean it, to not be faking a dry chuckle that says, *Look, I'm fine. I can handle this; it's not at all crushing or humiliating*. To feel actual amusement is to forget, to be elsewhere than in this made-for-television film starring Teri Hatcher, which is what I'm living. An unknown would play A, Stockard Channing would be Bunny. An upmarket production, as Christian would say.

I look into his blind-man's-blue eyes. I could marry Christian if he weren't like a brother to me. It seems tawdry to fantasize about a second husband before I'm officially divorced from the first. Also I deduce: Divorce is snakebite. One's next thought should not be, Where am I going to find another *snake*?

And Then What

The next day, while we are all driving to the children's shoe store, I ask A if he picked out his mommy before he was born.

"Yes."

I ask if he picked out his daddy before he was born.

"Yes."

He is so small and big and poignant and gentle and funny and the gift of what must be some kind of deity. He is a reason for not giving up, not even later on.

A asks what today is. "Friday, my baby," I say.

He goes on asking what we would be doing this weekend, and into the next week.

"You will be with your friends at preschool half a day."

"And then what?" he asks.

"You will be with your daddy for two days."

"And then what?"

"And then you will be with your friends and then you will be with your daddy ANOTHER two days."

"A whole family?" A says, very softly.

I think I have misheard. "What did you say?"

"A whole family," A says, staring out the car window, hugging his elbows.

I do not know how to answer, so I repeat how much we all love A, and I silently wish N under a steel girder. In the passenger seat, Christian smiles, his teeth set on edge as though he is encased in ice.

When we arrive home, Christian stretches out his long, tanned arm and points to the careful row of self-help divorce literature on my bookshelf. He makes the same grimace he made in the car.

"This shit has got to go," he announces.

We pile the books into sturdy cardboard packing crates: more charity for the Cerebral Palsy Society.

Christian ushers me to his laptop computer, to fill the sizeable hole on the shelves where the old books were. Together we agree that there are few tableaus more pathetic than a woman poring over a plethora of self-help books, while in a small café across town her husband is sharing a bottle of Pouilly-Fuissé and fettuccini Alfredo with a beautiful woman, fondling her fish-net knee and making careful plans to escape his life. We counteract all of this with the online purchase of anti-propaganda treatises.

Let the record state that I have all new books, now, hurtling to me from a warehouse in Michigan. They are:

Crazy Time
Dumped
The Rise and Fall of the Third Reich
Interview with the Vampire
American Psycho
Smart Women Finish Rich
Fraud
Scum
Anne Sexton: The Complete Poems + Letters
Fear and Loathing in Las Vegas
Last Words: The Final Journals of William S. Burroughs
How to Spot a Bastard by His Star Sign
The Witches' Almanac
The Motorcycle Poems, by Diane Wakowski

Surprise

"I've got a surprise for you," Christian says. "A big surprise," he adds as he cradles his cell phone in my kitchen and scans the Sunday *New York Times*, which is dated tomorrow.

Christian has been in town for a week now, staying at the local bed-and-breakfast. He lets himself in with N's old key in the morning and makes coffee. Christian told me he was going virtual at his network executive job for a few weeks, he was going to be an offsite satellite, which means gone.

I am a bit concerned about Christian's surprise. Surprises, I feel now, are primarily a form of violence.

"Bambi's coming," Christian announces, in the tone of *Jesus is coming*. His eyes actually twinkle.

Bambi is the 1950s Airstream trailer that Christian has loved for so very long and truly; never looking to upgrade, his eye never wandering farther than a decorator named Alfredo, who had very subtly and slowly maximized and modernized the appeal of the tiny sleeping loft with its sweeping back window and drapes, the porthole windows, the banquette, the slim shower inlaid with vintage tiles, the screen door in filigreed galvanized steel with its silent implacable hinge, keeping insects at bay. A sweet steel pod, all curves and ovals, stamped with the red, white, and blue emblem that reads "Bambi" in a friendly script. Bambi possessed a powerful charm, a feeling of being part of the world but not of the world; half in and half out, and able to move swiftly at any time, able to respond. Somehow Alfredo had incorporated a screening area into the mini loft and made Bambi tax deductible as well.

I feel palpably blessed. I'll soon have a tiny environment on wheels, completely contained and yet portable. It is so beautiful and so intact that I am a bit better. I was wrong about surprises. I feel as though I would like to live in Bambi while a cordial deaf-mute in white drove A and me around the country.

"Also, I've got a new driver," Christian announces.

"What happened to Gideon?"

"He's moving on to publishing," Christian replies. "Gideon's brilliant; you should have seen him at Shutters Hotel reception. He could will a suite. Just will it. Full ocean view."

I grunt.

"They're bastards there, too," Christian adds cheerfully.

"I know that," I say, thinking: *I used to work and travel, before I married and had a baby and a divorce and my life basically ended.*

"You're just on sabbatical," Christian says, reading my thoughts.

"They always put me in the dungeon rooms at Shutters. I had a view of a concrete patio. I was looking up at patio furniture," I say.

"Well, it's all over *now,* baby," Christian says.

We laugh a quick bark, as though seeing a tornado moving away.

"I'm lucky. I know that," I say, and I do. I am furious and outraged and heartbroken and lucky. I really do need a savior. But instead of asking for what I want, I ask about Bambi, which is fairly close to what I want.

"So who's the new driver?"

"The Betty Lady. Also known as Bill Coopersmith. But his friends call him the Betty Lady, or sometimes the Beebe," Christian replies.

"A man named Betty is bringing the Airstream," I say.

"Yes. Usually he does makeup for our daytime dramas, but he says he wants a break from the whole L.A. thing. He wants to just be."

"Does he dress?" I think this is the correct verbiage.

"Rarely. It's just all too much, it got too big. It's a tremendous amount of work, I don't know if you know that. Hours of makeup and costuming and then the thing itself, like being Tammy Faye Bakker every night. But he still does it for occasions."

"Is this an occasion?" I ask.

"We'll see . . . ," he says. "You never know with the Betty Lady. He'll just take my room here in town, at the B&B. It's all been arranged. . . . It was Gideon's last official act." Christian looks around the room as if expecting his belongings to materialize. Then he says, "This is exactly what I've needed: a reason to get out of the office."

"Yes. I'm sure that must be hell for you," I note dryly.

Christian never announces himself or asks permission. I find it endearing. I feel I've had too many appointments, or just one long one. And Christian has taken off. I can watch him unfold, like an umbrella, and then he's gone, off into the conceptual landscape. I know now that Christian will be staying on, and I'm relieved, although I was unaware I needed him to stay.

"What about the fall season?" I ask.

"It's a catastrophe. You won't believe how bad it is. In the end I think one person was almost killed. A helicopter."

Christian's eyebrows rise, emphasizing the closeness of his call.

"Very bad mongambo. No, I'm afraid the fall season is dead. I tried, but I failed. Probably all my fault. What could I do, fire everyone?

"They had nothing. Nothing." Christian sighs.

"That's not good," I say, trying to sound sorry, but it is very difficult to feel sorry for Christian.

"Well, it happens. It's like nature's way of clearing the forest."
"Oh . . . ?"

"The velvet hammer . . . ," Christian says ominously. "New York . . . ," he intones.

I reflect on this evidence of other people being harmed in other places, and feel slightly less alone.

"It's probably best," Christian says, ". . . they all just scurry over to Fox, anyway. Nothing's permanent. *Nothing*."

"Thanks for the update, Christian. Thank God you're here."

"I *know*," he says with real sincerity.

Christian adjusts a pillow beneath his smooth head, which bears no scent. No scent whatsoever. I am not exactly sure that I have even ever seen Christian perspire. Perhaps he simply has no reason to, and so doesn't. He seems to have an almost tangible familiarity with the world.

"Aren't you worried about your job?" I ask.

"Actually, I wouldn't mind getting fired. But I don't think it will happen."

It is clear to me that Christian has become an untouchable.

This would be like him; he has always been agonizingly vulnerable to any sort of success. And not just an untouchable, he's an untouchable in The Industry, as some preposterously insist on calling it. This means he has a good track record, nobody hates his guts, and that he has serious dirt on someone. He knows everyone who is leaving and everyone who is staying.

How nice that must be, I think. *Just to know.*

"And if anything big happens, which it will," Christian says, "I am just a phone call away. At the appropriate times, say once a day around six o'clock, when it's too late to change anything, anyway, and they've begun to hose down the blood. I can concept here . . . think about the bigger picture."

"Basically just get paid to fuck around until something changes," I finish the thought for him.

"That's true, but only in a sense," Christian says, and falls asleep on the sofa. He has occasional narcolepsy.

A pilgrimage to the ordinary and the squalid on the modern domestic front: I know he was thinking along those lines, and that someday in the not too distant future I may see a version of this whole ishkibibble on a national situation comedy or drama. It doesn't concern me. In fact if it happened, my only regret now would be that I might have to claim it as intellectual property if the divorce drags out.

War Crime Evidence

Bambi has arrived, is nestled in my driveway like a trim silver space capsule. Within one day of explaining the situation to Christian (and the Betty Lady, whom I take into my complete confidence based on instinct and the fact that he was wearing a sundress and pigtails when we met), the three of us are assembling the war crime evidence. That one of us happens to be a six-foot-four on-again/off-again transvestite only increases my sense of comfort in numbers.

The Betty Lady says, "Go to the American Express year-end statement. That's the mother lode."

"It is an invasion of privacy. In a way," I murmur as the Betty Lady upends a drawer onto N's home office floor.

"American Express: Don't leave your wife without it. Membership has its rewards, bitches. Bring me the phone bills. All of them." The Betty Lady issues commands. He has a heavy five o'clock shadow and is wearing sweatpants and a Yankees T-shirt.

"N is going to go ballistic when he sees this. . . ." I survey the mounting disarray in N's once-pristine office.

"*You get what you give*, we will tell his sorry, selfish ass." The Betty Lady has spoken. I detect a Bronx accent.

"But," I demur, "it will make the other woman say, 'See? She IS a jealous and paranoid and pushy wife.'"

The Betty Lady rips open a cell phone statement with a nail file and, without looking up at me, says, "Let me tell you something, honey. In my experience? The only thing they care about is what they see in the mirror each morning and WINNING . . . or their perception of winning."

"I love you . . . ," I say to the Betty Lady. He ignores me and leafs through N's credit card statement. "Dolce and Gabbana, anyone?" he calls out in a loud voice, like a train porter.

Dolce & Gabbana?

I told everyone I was quitting smoking, but I'm sucking hard on a Winston Light. I need to smoke several more cigarettes right away. I may need to *eat* the cigarettes.

Penis

I may now fully engage in the fact-seeking stage. If I choose, I can be Inspector Javert to N's Jean Valjean. I am replete with stamina in finding out every single fact I can about this whole affair.

Yet, I think, do I want to pull that thread? Do I want to unleash the truth, unravel deceit, and kill reality, as I've known it? It is irreparable, if I do, from the moment we met until now. It is long. If I discover too much that is false about what I thought my past was, Time will be skewed even further. I already have a poor connection with the present. Example: I have no sense of what day it is. It's better.

On the evening news, a head-scarfed woman visits her husband in prison, weeping and bringing him lunch meat and cigarettes. The sign posted in the prison visiting area reads:

NO KISSING
NO HUGGING
NO HANDSHAKES

A seems reflective also. He asks if I have a penis. I explain, all very technical and politically correct.

"Yes or no?" A says. This boy gets right to the point. I have much to learn from this boy.

"No," I say.

At dusk in Mill Valley, I sign the equity loan documents. They say, *Suzanne Finnamore. An unmarried woman.* Tabula rasa. Shocking.

So shocking, that television is my new best friend. Especially the old reruns I've videotaped from *Entertainment Tonight Weekend*. They announce that Liza Minnelli has married. She announces on *ETW* that she is planning to hang her nine-foot wedding train on her bedroom wall, to help her remember her event. *Save the zipper bag!* I say out loud.

Their live celebrity nuptial music included "Walk On By," by Dionne Warwick, and "One Bad Apple," by Donny Osmond.

In other *ET* news, Princess Stéphanie of Monaco and her boyfriend the Circus Owner are splitting up after over a year. He is still married, for one thing.

ANNOUNCER: *In the end the princess and her three children apparently never adjusted to living in a circus trailer. . . .*

Then I watched a *Sopranos* video. Then I leave a message for N at his office.

"Hello. Yes. You left A's raincoat in your car Saturday? That's cool. Look, try to hang on to this new raincoat I bought him today. We had a good day, by the way. We took a bath and I gave him a haircut. Regarding you and your new girlfriend, She Who Doesn't Exist You Swear To God? *Fuck you.*"

It feels good. But the good feeling doesn't last. It is thin, a cheap sweater. No way to take back the words, either. Not that I would. I am like Tony Soprano that way.

On Saturday, the devil once again entered my body. N came to pick up A for a visit. I made them a picnic lunch of thyme-roasted chicken, potato salad, fresh pears, and cheeses. Then I sent them off, having carefully groomed: a crisp white polo shirt, tanned skin, tight black running shorts, and new Nikes. When they return, N jocularly exclaims, "Wow, that chicken was great, thanks for making it."

"You're welcome," I say. Then I announce that the refinance had gone through. N starts to look uncomfortable.

"I was wrong about the appraisal on the house," I say.

Silence.

Then I smile and say, "It wasn't eight hundred K. It was a million two."

N and I paid $279,000 for our house when we were married.

His face caves in. He says, "I don't want to talk to you anymore. I don't like you."

He roars off in his Japanese sport-utility vehicle.

The settlement is more or less chugging along. I had waited all this time to tell him how financially secure I was, at least on paper. Money is a great god to N.

"He cannot STAND it that I am not curled up in a fetal position under the freeway," I say later to Christian as we eat fish tacos.

Christian comments, "I think he will do something crazy soon. He's revving up."

"How do you know? How best to ensure his nervous breakdown?" I ask.

"Keep going," Christian says. "Just go on as if nothing has happened. We all hate that."

"How do you handle things with Anita?" I ask, regarding his ex wife.

"I never write the alimony check. I never see her. Also? I never really loved her, and she never loved me."

"Ah," I say. This now makes absolute perfect sense.

The Shell Game with Jesus

The Betty Lady points out that I have Customized Outgoing Messages based on caller ID information. He seems disappointed that there aren't more features on my phone, but perks up at the suggestion that he take over the entire project.

For N's telephone calls, there is a new outgoing message on my answering machine:

"I'm here right now, so please leave a message at the sound of the tone."

The Betty Lady imitates my voice very well.

"This is going to get a lot of recognition," Christian comments from the kitchen. "But how do you see it playing out?"

They set up a system with a microrecorder and six different messages to play, in my own faux voice, if N calls. I have a choice of six different replies to any given question, thereby removing the need to speak to N. This is necessary because when I try to speak to N, invariably rage creeps up from my toes and within minutes I become Martha in *Who's Afraid of Virginia Woolf?* pinwheeling my arms around and slamming the phone.

Six outgoing digital responses seem a wonderful idea, an array of options. They are:

I'm here right now, so please leave a message at the sound of the tone.
Now isn't a good time for me.
There's somewhere else I have to be.
I can't talk now. When can you talk?
When are you seeing A next?
Contact your lawyer and have him contact me.

I do not have a divorce lawyer on retainer. I see no reason to pay someone to give me something I don't essentially want. I simply will not sign anything I do not agree to. Bunny and

Christian know everything about divorce, so this is a workable plan and not the bald lunacy it seems on the surface, the kind of thing that would destroy most other women and leave them penniless and bereft. N has a lawyer, the very best lawyer, J. Spikenard of the embossed letterhead. Any lawyer I could hire would crumble like phyllo dough beneath the weight of the Kentfield lawyer. So I will do without.

Oddly enough, this plan seems to work. Both Spikenard (a man who looks like Ichabod Crane in a Zegna suit and without the braid) and N feel unchallenged and all-powerful. A very dangerous feeling, as I know.

The Betty Lady and I return once more to the drive-through for the KFC Popcorn Chicken, something Christian says is *heart-breaking*. We hoist the fragrant bag up to the tree house, along with a two-liter bottle of Diet Dr Pepper.

We share a midnight joint in the tree house. I try to analyze my reality with the Betty Lady, who is so far removed from reality as to be able to offer a keen, long-lens perspective. I ask, "What went wrong? Last time I checked, we were okay. A was born, now this."

The Betty Lady explains love and splitting up: "It's like playing the shell game with Jesus. You can't figure anything out; it's best not to try. You'll just humiliate yourself." He is attending to a buttermilk biscuit as he says this, drenching it in the honey that comes in small plastic packets with the picture of the Colonel on them.

"Betty, just let me ask you one thing," I say to him. "As a man."

"What?" He looks accused. Tries ineffectually to wipe the honey from his hands. I'm distantly aware that I am asking marital advice from Trannie the Pooh, who is unnerved by anything that happens in his own hundred-acre woods. Yet this also qualifies him for simple truths.

"Do you think N is obsessed over someone else? Is it serious?"

Betty Lady looks at me with great caring, shaking his head in a negative response, back and forth, back and forth. Quiet relief furls over my body, as I know he would never lie to spare my feelings.

"Of course it is," he says.

I drink this fact in. Suck all the meat off a drumstick, throw the bone.

In the dark I can see the head of the joint glowing against the Betty Lady's face.

"In the sixties, when I ran off to the forest and smoked a spliff, I felt I was striking a blow for the Revolution," the Betty Lady notes.

"For me, it's sloth," I say. "Hedonistic sloth and escapism."

"Right," the Betty Lady says. Then he looks at me and says, "You really are losing weight. I can see it through the shoulders."

I smile, hugging my knees. "It probably won't come to this, but will you beat him up for me?"

"Just give me the sign."

"Okay," I say. "It could be any time."

"I know. Just remember the sign."

"What's the sign?"

The Betty Lady makes a peace sign with two fingers.

Interest from the Mother-in-Law

Françoise is not at all pleased with the new outgoing message system.

"What izzat about?" she shrieks into the telephone. "Suzanne!?"

Françoise always sounds as if she is walking through the dark and I have the flashlight, and also the caviar and champagne.

"I'm here, Françoise. Sorry."

"Av you gone insane?" Françoise asks. "Are you drinking? I don' know . . . ," she muses.

"No, and yes," I say. There is a wonderful sense with Françoise that now that her son has done this, anything pretty much goes, on my end of the telephone.

"Don' drink. You'll get fat," Françoise pronounces.

"Don't worry," I say. "Terror is keeping the weight off. I'm fucking miserable."

"And don' swear. You sound like a prostitute."

"Thank you," I say. "That's the nicest thing anyone's said to me all day."

"How is A? Iz he all right?"

"A is fine," I say.

"I miss 'im so much," she says.

And I know she does. She visits every year on her birthday, and was only in town for two days this last time.

"A is fine," I say again.

Silence. She wants details.

"He is reading books upside down, playing regularly and nicely with his daddy, and eating everything in sight, including two Styrofoam peanuts I caught him with yesterday, which he was chewing on like tobacco."

"'E could die. 'E could choke. Be careful," Françoise says.

"I'm trying," I say, having purged the entire property line of Styrofoam peanuts.

"Did you get my package?" Françoise asks.

"Yes," I say. "Merci! *Très jolie . . .*"

Françoise sent A a blue and white seersucker blazer and some off-white Polo khakis. A looks like F. Scott Fitzgerald in this new outfit. Tremendous.

"Thank you for the earrings," I say. "You're too kind. Stop spending your money on us."

"I can't 'elp it," Françoise admits.

"Oh, I know," I say. "I have mail-order issues."

"Be careful with your money," Françoise says. "You don't want to lose za house."

"I know," I say. Right again.

"Your houz is nizzer than where N lives now," she says. Tipping her hand, showing me some face cards.

"Is it?" I ask.

"Yes," Françoise says. "Much, much nizzer. Iz new place is boxy."

Boxy. Fantastic.

"I love you, Françoise," I say.

"Don't drink too much," she says, hanging up.

The Buyout

Today the call came from the loan company, officially approving my buyout loan. I feel momentarily victorious.

The final settlement, I imagine, will also be very fair. I'll keep everything beginning with consonants (house, baby, dining room set, jewelry, dishes, dresser, bed), and N will keep everything beginning with vowels (armoire, umbrellas), because he is basically a good man and riddled with guilt.

This is turning out to be more and more of a comfort. We are a far cry from the first bit of time when I wept and said, *I don't care, take everything*. We are in a whole other state.

N, never used to giving a millimeter, is whining constantly about The Hole he is going to end up with. His prophecies of Chapter 11 are now commonplace.

"Divorce is expensive," I say in a lilting tone. *Especially the way you do it,* I don't add.

On the metaphysical front, the burning of sage is unsuccessful. House reeks of doom, and now sage too.

Telling

Last night I dreamt N was swinging a switchblade, one with a very long blade, uncommonly long, gruesomely long, as long as a vampire's fingers, swinging it back and forth and almost cutting my throat each time, and I knew if I would only keep silent it would not happen, I would live. Telling is death, in the dream. Even in life itself (and I think this in the dream, am aware of the real world as well as the switchblade), restraining orders don't stop anyone from showing up at one's house with a rifle, or a knife. An ax, a chain saw. A homemade bomb, wrapped like cake in tinfoil.

In the past I was always very careful not to show the outside world what was strange in N, his way of looking straight through everyone and doing nothing or doing everything. I took it on without anyone asking me to.

During our marriage, N and I had split the grocery expenses. At the end of the month we tallied it all up; it was a lot of trouble. We both wanted to make sure things were even.

I cheated. Not in the addition of the grocery receipts, but in the way I threw things into the grocery cart that had no business being there. The entire Olay Regenerist product line, *People* magazine, novels. Barrettes. I would like to go back and throw in a Cessna.

Other memories.

N was in New York on business. I rearrange all our furniture.

I throw away one of his Liberace shirts, cackling as I stuff it deep in the garbage bin.

Later he calls from his hotel to say it's twenty-nine degrees and he's freezing. He blames me for this.

I had told him it would be in the forties.

"It said so on AOL," I say. "It said high of forty-six."

"I should have brought my topcoat," he complains.

"I guess so," I say. A resentful air wells between us. It fills the little holes on the receiver.

"It took me half an hour to get a cab," he says. He says it as though he has just come back from Donner Pass with one leg, the other of which ended up on the buffet.

I do not say I am sorry. That sort of thing came later, apologizing for the weather.

"It might snow," he says.

I had wanted badly to laugh, but I didn't. I knew then not to ever laugh. *No:* I knew when to laugh and when not to laugh. It is a measure of relief to be free of these constraints. I'd been living with a Third World despot with good suits and a BlackBerry and had not even known it.

To keep myself from harming or calling N and to stave off the rage and despair, I focus on my extraordinary son, drinking mid-range Chardonnay every night after he is asleep, and making a barrage of late-night mail-order retail purchases placed from the couch. The couch has officially become my second battle station. I am angry and I have credit. And I'm all blackened inside; I should wear a pointy witch hat around Larkspur as I go to the bank and drop A off at day care. It would be more honest.

I loathe this feeling. It is like falling in love, only the opposite. I know now with blind certainty that no matter what, eventually marriage is just two financially interdependent strangers staring across the kitchen table at each other. They each have backpacks slung across their bodies, containing their sexual and romantic history and unresolved issues and family memories. And there's nothing but cold cereal, because the days of flaky croissants and foamy cappuccino are over. Reality reclines on top of the refrigerator, leering down with a wry yet tender expression. And one day it all just collapses and the backpacks are hauled away to another kitchen table. I've blown past Bitter and am already in the heart of Apathy.

I charged a gorgeous Asian water fountain thing from Vivre mail order. There are also boxes from Neiman Marcus, Nordstrom, Amazon, Rue de France, and Saks in my foyer. I like watching them collect, these things I can in no way afford.

When Snails Mattered

"The snails are eating the primroses," N once said, standing in our rain-drenched yard.

Then he said, "I can't believe this is my main concern."

I remember how we laughed at this in our small postcard garden, and then I picture N and Thing Woman together, laughing and laughing. Right now I would very much like to set fire to a large dry structure just to hear the crackling sounds and feel the heat on my skin. I could spray gasoline on the fire with a hose.

When snails mattered. Why can't we just go back to when snails mattered? I curl up in Bambi and wait for the pain to pass.

Christian is on his laptop, trawling through the Fine Hotels of the World Internet site, saying the features out loud:

"All within the vocabulary of the Arts and Crafts movement . . .

"The spa's Oz-like reception lounge . . .

"Guest rooms survey the Pacific Ocean from broad, craftsman-style porches . . .

"Jacuzzi bathtub with leather pillow headrest . . .

"Ian Schrager hotels . . . Only six hundred fifty dollars . . . ," Christian remarks. "That's not bad.

"Hot naked girl in bed. Can't see all of her. Lexington and Sixty-third, hmmm.

"Wait a minute. I just want to View All Rooms.

"The standard room looks like shit. Hideous headboard.

"Ahh, the one-bedroom suite looks okay. . . ."

I feel I'm listening to the ocean, so soothing is Christian. He and A are keeping my world upright with sheer molecules and whipped air.

"This is my pornography," Christian says.

I light a cigarette and we both lay back and watch the ceiling.

Betrayal Olympics

They definitely deserve the Bronze, N and Thing Woman—
and I feel the Silver may not be out of the picture.

N calls today from his cell phone: "With my permission," he
would like to take A to Disneyland.

"You don't need my permission for anything, N," I lilt. "How
are you?"

"Terrible," N says.

"Huh," I say, as though looking at something distracting
through the window as he spoke.

I very casually tell him I had been thinking about Thing
Woman and him, how it all began, the planning and the details—
what a thrill they must have gotten.

He says, "It wasn't like that. . . ."

I laugh out loud, a jolly laugh.

"Anywho," I muse aloud, "thinking about how all the pieces
fit together now? I realize that the two of you are even more
contemptible than I originally thought."

"I don't want to hear this," he says.

"Of course not," I demur.

"I'm not going to talk about my personal life. I don't want to
play your game," he says.

When he finally asks about A, I tell him he had a fever last
Friday night but is fine now. N makes a kind of groaning noise.

"I don't want to hear this," he says. But apparently he does, because he stays on the line.

I say, "Well, A does love and miss you, and I live with that every day, but to share it all with you would just make you sad, N. It would make it harder for you to do what you have to do, so I jes' keep it to myself. It's better dat way."

I have slipped into 1930s MGM picaninny dialect without knowing why.

"You've made your opinion of me quite clear, Massa. You've made your decision, and so that's that," I drawl matter-of-factly.

N spews promises, how he will never miss child support payments or his visitations with A.

"We'll see," I say warmly. "After all, it don't do to look too far into the future . . . never know what'll happen. . . ."

"Everyone's going to be fine," N says, sounding relieved. Everyone meaning himself and his girlfriend and, parenthetically, A.

"Honey? I wish both y'all the happiness you so richly deserve," I say.

"I'm not going to talk about my personal life," N says.

Is he starting this conversation all over again? I shrug and hang up. *Lordy.*

Let It Go

It was decided that a girls' dinner party would be held in honor of my forty-first birthday. Lisa plus Bunny and three or four women I worked with at the ad agency, each of them married. This does not escape my notice, it is a context. I resent the fact of a context; my social status has shifted and no one is going to acknowledge it, that's certain. I'm expected to be Brave and Rise Above. I dress for the role; I must look far better now than I did when I was married. I must look pulled together into a nice tight Hermès knot of self-containment. I don't make the rules; I just do my best to follow them.

Okay, I think. *Right, I can do this. I will rise above. He's nothing. I have A, that's everything. Right. Got it.*

A man at the bar buys me a drink while I am waiting. He has on a raincoat even though it is not raining; this sticks in my emotional craw. He also has thin wire glasses and a broad, tanned face, the kind of face that could pass security checkpoints.

He says, "I am susceptible to beauty."

"Thank you," I say. "Actually this is the first time I've worn makeup in a month, or shoes with heels."

"Really?" he says, looking straight through me to my vagina.

He's not all bad. For a crazed moment I thought about giving him my card, but then I notice that he has guzzled two scotch rocks in ten minutes. I don't go out with alcoholics. I don't go out with anyone, actually. He hasn't said anything since my remark about not wearing makeup. It all seems excruciatingly complicated and humiliating and when the women arrive I am gratefully swept up into their perfume and clattering heels.

We all enjoy a fine dinner at the Buckeye Roadhouse. I have oysters bingo and pepper-crusted filet mignon with scalloped potatoes and sautéed greens, and then we all share three pieces of coconut cream pie drizzled with chocolate.

Dinner was delicious and I am in fine form until at the end when someone got soulful—the subject of Thing Woman came up and then the woman next to Lisa, Brianna, takes my hand and says, "You need to let it go."

I look down at my hand, very slowly, as though someone has placed a scorpion on it. My brain is attempting to register the fact that a woman is holding my hand and telling me to do something, employing the dulcet tones that one reserves for the mentally ill.

This has never happened before. No girlfriend ever held my hand before, I think. Does Brianna think I am some kind of a eunuch now?

"Let the feelings move through you and away," Brianna says, raising her chin to indicate the direction of Away. Her malachite and silver Hopi earrings twist in the candlelight.

I drop Brianna's hand and rise up in my cane chair like a cobra and announce that not only was I not letting it go for the foreseeable future, but that actually? Actually I wished Thing Woman a venereal disease.

Horrified looks all around the table—cries of "No, no, it will backfire!!!!" from everyone except Lisa, who is laughing, and Bunny, who is reading the small square leather-bound dessert wine menu.

I point a finger into the air and say, "I wish her a disfiguring boil."

More cries of "BACKFIRE BACKFIRE."

"You're bigger than that," Brianna insists.

"No, I am not," I say quite clearly. There is an echo going on. Lisa is motioning furiously for the check. The Last Supper flashes across my mind, and I laugh and turn to Brianna and say, "Forgive me, I know not what I do." Then I run to the bathroom and vomit. Damned *martinis*.

How can people be so misled by the appearance of poise and success? I wonder, washing my shoes in the restroom sink. I am not bigger than that. I am smaller than anyone can imagine. I am an amoeba.

Simple Solutions

Lisa and I are at Mel's on Lombard Street. Two single moms are sitting next to us: two daughters with two plain middle-aged women without wedding bands. Patsy Cline's "Crazy" is available on the jukebox. I keep my quarters to myself.

"When they run out and file? It's always another woman," I say. "I can't believe I didn't get that right away."

"How is A holding up?" Lisa asks.

"He's okay. But he rarely does his belly laugh."

A has a spectacular belly laugh.

Lisa says idly, "The more we talk about it, the more I just want to have my brother run him over with a rental van."

"What about forgiving thy trespassers?" I ask; Lisa is religious, a fact only I and a few others know.

There is a long silence as we both sip chocolate milk shakes.

"God is great and God is good," Lisa says. "But where are the Apache attack helicopters when you need them?"

"I know." I sigh.

Today I am truly looking for reasons. Reasons to not commit a random crime and spend some time in jail, just reading. Lisa looks up from her patty melt and immediately says, "Okay, SORRY, but did you ever have anything again like the beans?"

The Beans. The Beans of legend. Senior year of high school.

"We used to make a special trip to Richmond, just to get the beans . . . ," I recite. "One time I got Bunny to come with us. Bunny didn't believe driving to Richmond was worth the beans."

"Right. And I told Bunny, when you taste them you will know," Lisa, who knows the correct response, says. "I remember I paid."

"They served them in quart Styrofoam containers with special lids. Cheese melted on top. And we didn't have spoons," I say.

"I was driving us back, and Bunny's in charge of holding the beans. I never imagined what would happen in the car . . . ," Lisa reflects.

"And Bunny can't wait. And there are no spoons. So she uses the plastic lid as a scoop," I say. "She should have been prepared. As if for the Holy Regalia."

"And Bunny is scooping, and I am screaming, 'Fucking beans!!!!! Fucking beans!!!!!'" Lisa cries.

"So we made it back a quart shy."

"They were beans that will never be equaled."

"To call it a refried bean just doesn't do it justice."

"Even when we moved on to college, Bunny would force us to go buy beans."

"Yes. We used to sing, because there was no radio in the Corolla . . ."

"'Indian Sunset.' 'If I Fell.' 'Dust in the Wind.'"

"Thank you," I say. "I'd forgotten about the beans."

"Well, Jesus. Wake up," Lisa says. "I love you."

"I love you too, and thank you for the beans."

"They weren't my beans. They were just the Beans," she says. "It was luck."

I'd almost forgotten about luck.

Start Small

I need to remove myself from the psychic sphere of my mother-in-law, Françoise.

I am ranting on the phone to Bunny as I peel carrots into the sink until they are orange toothpicks.

"Aren't there laws about this sort of thing? Why do you lose the husband but keep the constant vigil of his mother? This is clearly abuse. Built right into the system."

"Françoise wants to help. But I am forty and she talks to me as if I have just broken my hymen. She is flinging bromides and prayers to me, lobbing helpful suggestions like cans of okra to someone without a can opener deep in a foxhole with explosions all around, and snipers in the fucking trees."

"Oh, I agree totally," Bunny says. "I never wanted to share the limelight with her in the first place."

"Can we please just talk about me?" I say. "On the one hand, she is offering both verbal and written advice on how to dress, exercise, and of course the obvious: how to feel."

"Feel?" Bunny says. "How can you be expected to feel? You're a mother now, for God's sake."

"I could deal with Françoise if I still had the phone to occasionally hand back to N. But now he is gone. I've got the hand grenade. It's live. It's eighty years old and ticking."

"But you usually get along so well with Françoise. What's she doing different?" Bunny shrewdly asks.

"Primarily, Françoise is asking me to *forgive* N."

Bunny gasps. "What did you say to her?"

"I told her, 'I think I should start small, by not wishing him dead.'"

"Well done," Bunny says.

"PLEASE," I say, and hang up with a flourish.

Gift

Much like trains in India, grief is a circular, irrational process with no discernible rhythm or timetable. Here it comes, there it goes. I don't need Nadine to tell me this, but I do tell her, in case she herself doesn't know.

"Sometimes amidst the pain surges, the emotional dumping? I get a wave of pleasure and freedom that takes me from the toes up. And I am constantly reminded that it's my great good fortune to have somehow kept A in this unraveling," I announce.

"I know," Nadine says, a tiny smile playing on her lips. "I see this a lot: It's like they steal the silverware and leave the Monet."

A has humor, cuteness, honesty, and he looks stunning in yellow pants and no top.

"Also . . . it's hard to get any really good existential dread going when A is in the room singing 'HAVE YOU SEEN THE MUFFIN MAN?'" I comment.

Nadine says, "Exactly."

I feel I'm getting hell of gold stars in my grief therapy. A is the best Christmas gift of all, and virtually free. Unlike Nadine.

And now, dusk. A's in his bedroom playing alone and I am lying on my bed as he softly berates, chortles, advises his stuffed rabbits, and conducts his daily business. To my amazement and great, bittersweet joy, I can hear in him every reason I fell in love with his father—everything, like a second sonata to a first. All the lovely unspoiled good of N, bubbling forth from his son, unlooked for, oozing up from a well of genealogy and fate. I can manage to misplace my husband, but this flesh is chained to mine. I will always be reminded of the marital loss, but I have the benefits of the entire play, the witness of the evolution, the new art. I see the magic every day; I live with the sorcerer in yellow pants. N gets pieces and stems of A, random and marred by guilt.

The next day he comes to collect some items from the garage. I can see the avarice bubbling up inside him as he strolls into the two-car garage. Boxes that are unopened drive him mad. What's this? What's that? He is working toward an inventory that has no chance of benefiting him. When he finds the set of solar-powered walkway torchlights, he gasps. Then the Coleman stainless-steel cooler with the lifetime guarantee. He would like to pick up the whole garage and move it to his new square, move it on with his life; I see that in his eyes. They are not glistening at me; they are glistening at the George Foreman Grill, still in its box. As he walks out, he slips a few things into his coat pockets. The pettiness of it slays me. The small spray bottle of ArmorAll, the rubbing compound. Some bungee cords.

How, from where we began, have we come to this?

Satan's Elves

In continuation of intestinal self-destructive mode, I drive through Burger King. A sits in the back like a sultan, demanding French fries with cat shit (ketchup). Waxing maternal, I decide he needs protein, so I order a chicken nugget pack for my son. A takes one bite and starts screaming like a whistle. It turns out the food handlers have temporarily lapsed in their efficiency. It's a jalapeño cheese popper. Outraged, I take a bite myself: terrifyingly delicious. I save the rest for the cocktail hour. Reheated in the microwave, they are even better than I had originally estimated. Lisa agrees: The jalapeño cheese poppers are Satan's elves.

Writing every day again on the produce campaign assignment is good busywork to avoid feelings of doom and self-loathing. N is coming on Saturday with cheap Irish movers to get his furniture and final boxes. Arguments over who gets the pepper grinder, garlic press, etc. I think, This will be the last horrible thing I have to go through, until I meet someone else and the whole travesty begins again. I myself bear a sign that reads DON'T DATE ME, I CHAIN-SMOKE, I'M BITTER, AND I INCLUDE GRABBY TODDLER, and this has dramatically decreased my social life. I have resigned myself to a lifetime of jalapeño poppers and cheap wine and *Frasier* reruns.

Why has no one proposed yet? I do feel bad about that. Lowering standards by the minute but still nothing. Recently I decided the contractor working on the construction site down the street looked like Harrison Ford. I slowed my car down and tried to look available, despite baby seat in the back and Elmo sunshade. Then today he looked like Ray Liotta to me. I know my vision is impaired and cannot be trusted with even the simplest tasks, much less dating. Not that I've come within talon distance of a man.

I say all this to my mother as we sit and eat nachos at Joe's Taco Lounge.

"God. I would have to run over the Ford/Liotta contractor to meet him: jump the curb, ruin my car, and chance arrest. Even running him over may not ensure an introduction. Maybe I could just clip him as he crosses the street? This would require keener eyesight than I apparently have. I would probably clip him into a coma."

Bunny nods, drinking a Tecate and doing a crossword puzzle.

"I'm just not sending out the right vibe lately. Perhaps the fact that I wear stained sweatpants and free T-shirts is holding me back. I just can't seem to get back into the intelligent-slut-for-hire outfits that lure men; even shoes with laces evade me. Plus my hair is Fran Lebowitz-esque. I think my eyes are getting closer together. I don't know."

"Pass the salt," Bunny says.

Dirt Bastard

N has been calling all day, leaving messages reinforcing about how he wants A for Christmas. He and Thing Woman are flying to Hawaii for Christmas, and they want to take A.

Yes. That will be happening any minute, I think to myself. Just step over my bloated corpse, and he's yours.

The moment I catch sight of his bald head, I accost Christian in my kitchen.

"So now he wants to reserve A for Christmas. Like a live lobster or something: 'Oh, that sounds good. I'll have one.' "

"Just say no," Christian says as he eats some tiny organic bananas from Ecuador that I've gotten free samples of; he has been ridiculing my ads, but he just loves the mini bananas. "One syllable. *No.* It's wonderfully freeing. I say it constantly."

I think about it for four hours, and then I relent and pick up the phone with a wearied sigh. When N answers, I say, "A is too young to be away from home on Christmas, and he will be here with my family, as per usual."

"I can make that difficult for you," N says.

"Yes, I'm sure you can. But why not let A have his tradition? After all, he has lost a father this year, YOU FUCKING DIRT BASTARD," I say, hanging up.

I feel I am seeing his true colors now. If he were a rock group, I'm certain that his name would be The Total Pricks. If he were an ant, I would step on him. Squash the fuck out of him.

"So," Lisa says, watching me from the trim Todd Oldham La-Z-Boy I impulse-purchased last week. "You handled that well, Lucretia."

Stocking

Christmas Eve. There's no way around it, it comes every single year right exactly on time. I rely on poetry and Charles Dickens and mulled wine. I am reading to A tonight; we are reading "The Night Before Christmas" when A suddenly says, "We'd better take Daddy's stocking down, because he's not going to be here tomorrow."

N is of course with Thing Woman in the Hawaiian Islands, for reasons unknown to the sentient world. I died a few emotional mother-deaths, seeing his stoicism.

eeeeeeeeeeeeeeeeeeee

I turn to A.

"Well, yes," I reply, "but then Santa Claus wouldn't be able to leave anything in Daddy's stocking. So we should probably leave it out over the chimney until, say . . . January twelfth."

A grimaces. "Allll riiiiigghhhtt . . . ," he says. His face is emptied of something.

I call N. I dial Hawaii with perfect composure.

"I know this is difficult for you to hear, but it is not your privilege to remain untouched—you need knowledge of the fact of A's grief in that you're not even around in the smallest slimmest thinnest sense for the holidays, not until the twelfth of January. Would a phone call have killed you? And how did I become your Jewish mother just now as I asked that? Oh, my."

"I have to go," N says. "I can't listen to this."

"This is terribly hard for him, N. You need to do something other than snorkel."

"You're probably making some of this up . . . ," he pivots. Now I've got the hot ball. No way.

"Oh, yes. This is my REAL calling, the fiction of inventing sad Christmas children . . . right. Just call him, okay?" I say, hanging up the phone and wishing once again for my trusty flamethrower.

Just One Question

Now that he's back from what seemed a protracted series of unprecedented luxury vacations, I must say it's difficult to see N so frequently. When A leaves the room, we talk, but not in an Earl Grey way, more like a Molotov cocktail way. One day, after they leave to go to the park, I sit quietly for five minutes. Then I careen out of the driveway, stop to put on my seat belt, breathe. Then I drive slowly to the park where N is watching A swing. I walk up to him, look him in the eye, and say, "There's something I need to ask you before I can move forward in my life."

Of course this is every man's dream question; he looked like a rapist who has just been handcuffed to a genitalia electric chair.

"I want you to tell me how you could have said and done what you did before you left."

There are tears slowly drifting into my nose from my eyes. I hold my ground.

"How could you do that to me?" I repeat. I don't have to itemize. He knows what I speak of.

Eventually N produces three answers, in this order:

1. "Because I am a complete rotter." I silently agree, but it's a cop-out: *I have maggots, therefore I am dead.*
2. "I was stressed at work and unhappy and we were always fighting . . . and you know I was just crazy. . . ."

I cut him off, saying, "You don't get to be crazy. You did exactly what you chose to do."

Which is true, he did. It is what he has always done. He therefore seems slightly puzzled at the need for further diagnosis, which may explain his third response:

3. "I don't know."

This, I feel instinctively, is the correct answer. How can I stay angry with him for being what he is? I was, after all, his wife, and I chose him. No coincidences, that's what Freud said. None. Ever.

I wipe my eyes on my sleeve and walk toward the truck, saying to his general direction, "Fine. At least now I know: You don't know."

I stop and turn around and fire one more question: a bullet demanding attention in the moment it enters the skin and spreads outward, an important bullet that must be acknowledged.

"What did you feel?"

After a lengthy pause, he answers. "I felt nothing."

And that, I realize too late, was not the whole truth, but was a valid part of the truth.

Oh, and *welcome to the Serengeti*. That too.

III
Bargaining

Love and war are the same thing,
and stratagems and policy are allowable
in the one as in the other.

—Cervantes

First Draft

My estranged husband and I are reviewing the first draft of the divorce settlement in his sport-utility vehicle outside the couples counseling office. It is a beautiful summer day that I cannot acknowledge, as I am falling off a precipice onto jagged snags of granite. Next to me N floats in a parachute of his own design: He wants the divorce, I don't. He pushed me, I fell. I plummet; he pulls the ripcord and feels a refreshing lack of weight or gravity.

Inside his car, we carp like a very old married couple as he attempts to read the legal papers aloud. "'Irreconcilable differences not solved by couples counseling,'" he reads, in his cool, precise, and technical voice. He should be on a wheelie little stool in an antiseptic examining room: *Crow's-feet not solved by chemical peel or laser.*

"Lies," I say of the papers. "Fucking lies." This is so Woody Allen. In fact, if I squint, I can almost see Woody Allen, slouching behind the car with a director's sight around his neck and saying, *That was dreadful. Make it smaller.*

It's not as though N tried very hard in couples counseling, during our first $180-an-hour go-round. He just sat there grimacing and polishing his bendable Japanese titanium eyeglasses and talking nicely about the therapist's shoes. And the therapist, another tall, pale man who obviously belonged to N's affluent-man club, seemed pleased, and answered the questions about his shoes. "Kenneth Cole," he said. I sat rearranging my insides and breathing very slowly, so as not to scream forth like a teakettle.

I struggled not to rage or weep because I didn't want to be embarrassed. I see now that not only should I have wept, I should have tied N's glasses in a bow until he spoke truth. That might have gotten the medicine ball rolling. I was despicably weak, but I can change. I can change in the months before our divorce is final, gaining style and presentation points and therefore placing in the Overall.

During last year's couples counseling, N never leaked the minor detail that he was having an affair. He just held his own counsel, all at $180 an hour.

Now it's our final couples counseling appointment, and only because we're performing a "relationship autopsy." Relationship autopsies are highly recommended now by people who know. The procedure promises something like clarity, or even *closure*, a word that has been abused and now banned. A relationship autopsy, exhuming the bodies and brains that we once were, poking about our hearts and checking for foreign substances and foul play, so as to gain knowledge and help one avoid future deaths.

"How do you feel, Suzanne, about the discovery of N's affair?" the marriage counselor asks.

"I feel covered in shit," I say.

Marriage counselor thinks: *Covered in shit. Right.*

Crosses his legs. Looks compassionate. Thinks of next appointment and does he have time to make a call to his hairstylist. Both he and N nod with solemnity and look down at their shoes. I am sure they are indifferent, are waiting for the hour to be up so they can procure more accessories to impress others with. There are more software programs to be cracked open, more marriages to dissect and dispose of. At $180 an hour. This is like paying gangsters for my own hit, and sitting around talking about it beforehand with creased, earnest faces. I've dreaded it every time.

They make you do it, marriage counseling. Society and the media make you do it. It's *the* ritual for the end of a marriage. You have to do it or they make you feel irresponsible and dishonest and lazy. The marriage is over; counseling is the eulogy. The relationship autopsy is the wake.

Finally the session is over. We emerge onto a sunny street, near the ocean. We experience a kind of adolescent freedom. We have successfully completed this one thing, together. He walks me to my car. Broad daylight, he walks me to my car. He opens the car door for me. Time moves backwards. He gets into the car, noticing how much longer my legs look now that I'm a stick figure. We commiserate on the ugliness of the legalese in the settlement. We hold hands, embrace. I am crying from the first draft and its content, and he is groping at my body—either to comfort me or gratify himself. There is no explaining it. This is not a normal divorce. Are there any? The overwhelming feeling is that we may still love each other; that chemistry runs like an underground cave. If I try, I can hear it, thrumming. But that may be jive, I know: Divorce is not akin to engagement. (Affairs are not jewelry, though they often lead to jewelry. In fact, I received quite expensive jewelry during our last Christmas together. Estate jewelry.) I can see my brain is reprogramming events. *Must watch out for my brain,* I resolve.

The next day. He calls. "Did you just call me?"

"No," I say flatly.

That must be one of your whores, I don't say. *Bitch whose teeth I would like to smash with a croquet mallet.*

Now that Christian has left and performed his emotional triage on me, I stay rather calm, more contained. I no longer blame Thing Woman or myself quite so much for N's leaving us. I look at him sometimes for an unguarded moment and see a tall, crooked man with yellowing teeth and a leer. I see new N. Bad N. Vulnerable to anyone with a vagina. I also see Good N, just a glimpse, here and there. And Noncommittal N, an extra in his own life, just hitting his marks and looking well pressed. He's become a whole group of people, a cache of ghosts tugging at my sleeve.

Good N was phenomenal.

Wrong

N and I are sitting together on my love seat reading the Sunday *New York Times* while A gets dressed for his visit. He is reading the book reviews to me. I love to be read to, it was one of N's indulgences that had slain me. He liked to read to me on the weekends, he fed me pieces of *The New Yorker*. I'd tilt my head up so I could see the cartoons by the pink light of the bedside lamp. I am experiencing a time warp and I want it to last forever. There is plenty of newspaper; it's delivered every Sunday. I may want to do this every Sunday, just for the hell of it, but the divorce will destroy even this small pleasure. *Everything must go.*

He has on a soft gray cashmere sweater from Costco. "Thirty dollars," he tells me, as though to prove he has no extra money lying around. Just those thirty dollars. This is known as Crying Poor, an innate and immediate response to the serving of divorce papers. Yearly incomes, exotic vacations, raises of any kind, or the sudden appearance of cars, boats, or motorcycles are not considered valid factors in the Crying of Poor: They can all be rationalized . . . they are gifts from secret benefactors or prizes won by lotteries or golf club raffles. Frequently, allowances are made for flat denial: *Yes, there is a Jaguar in my garage, but I have no idea where it came from.*

I also participate by not telling him about any incoming moneys, no matter how significant or exciting. If I won the lottery tomorrow, I would keep it to myself, in order to get the highest child support amount possible ordered by the court. Is this love? I wonder. Divorce is love's miscarriage, bloody and shot through with loss.

He puts both arms around me and squeezes hard, as though grief could be pushed out, toothpaste from a tube. I ask, "Is this wrong, what we're doing?"

"Probably," he says casually.

It is his casualness that gives me chills. Of course it's wrong. I know it's wrong, and I think I will know when to stop. I know that he won't stop. He is an animal. Once again, this now works in my favor instead of being a horror.

Meanwhile, I am back to string panties and the whole arsenal: When N dropped A off late this afternoon, I was lying in the sun on the front porch in underwear and a flimsy bra, my skin pressed against the warm wood.

He said hello, I said hello. I wore Persol sunglasses: a force field of invincibility. Then I simply and effortlessly stretched my hand out to N. I wanted that passionate, hard kissing sex, the kind that lasts for an hour. So I just took it. I beckoned him as one would a hot dog vendor at a ball game.

"I suppose I will never become a good and evolved person. Things just keep getting in the way," I say to Lisa later on the phone. "But I will say this. It made me feel like a woman again."

"It's *so* Gladys Knight," Lisa observes. She emits a great sigh, as if facing a room full of straw that she is expected to spin into gold. "So pedestrian, Suzanne. I can't see anything to it, and yet me being me and you being you, I actually do know why you are doing this."

"Why?" I ask. My God, a windfall in this informational deficit.

"You still need information. N is your Gordian knot, your Rubik's Cube," Lisa says. I hear the tinkle of ice on glass. "You will either undo the knot, figure it out, get bored, or toss him away in frustration."

"Couldn't it be much simpler? That I am just tired of driving A and myself everywhere, of doing it all alone? Couldn't I just want N back to drive once in a while?"

"You know, honey, there are people who will do that for money, instead of blood," Lisa says.

"I miss being a passenger," I reflect.

Lisa says, "With N, you will always be a passenger. He's not going to let that wheel go."

I completely agree with Lisa and continue to catapult straight toward my goal, which is to Get My Husband Back.

Hitchcock

We hold hands. We confide. We do all the things we are not supposed to do. We nefariously and covertly act like a normal, semidetached husband and wife. This is the irony. It's the new cheating.

We rarely talk about Thing Woman, and I can feel that she

doesn't truly exist. Like death, I can believe in her for other people but not for me personally. I erase her constantly in my mind. This thrills me no end. N's avoidance and emotional limitations are now to my advantage, instead of to my detriment. I use him: He now enjoys doing chores around the house. I use him like a hammer. Bam Bam Bam. I am trying to even the playing field. This fails. I can't pick up a hammer without getting hit.

Now I may want him back, as I have more or less all along. But now it's become war, versus simpering or bravado. I am also involved in the biggest bargaining project of all: the very final divorce settlement. My system is that I keep sending the agreement back to Joseph Spikenard, N's lawyer, unsigned, until I get what I want. I personally don't require a lawyer for this. Why should I pay someone pots of money for something I don't desire?

Last year I did meet with one attorney for an hour, and she told me everything I was entitled to and everything he was entitled to, and ran my Visa through a clackety plastic machine. Five hundred dollars. This cured me of lawyers forever. So I now know the laws of California divorce; it's medieval. During this phase, I am carefully and with master timing cobbling out the divorce settlement and child support verbally and then through a local notary with N. I must be subtle with N, until everything I can get for my son and myself is properly secured in my own name.

It all gets very Hitchcock. Everyone has something they want, a personal agenda, and there is much drinking of coffee, brandy, and smoking of cigarettes. Even though N has abandoned us and served me with divorce papers, winning still seems possible.

So last night, when N got tipsy and ran over a giant raccoon, I took full advantage of his temporary loss of power and control. And now here he is, all 195 lean pounds of him, sleeping on my futon. I savor his light snore, the smell of him. Earlier, he bared his hairy chest like a gorilla. Then we made love raucously.

What's odd is, I'd called him just minutes before he showed. I never call him at night, but that night, I felt driven. The fibrous strands of connection, still functioning.

He answered his cell phone and said, "Oh, it's you. I hit a raccoon with my car. I'm in a bar now."

There was a pause.

"Well," he said sarcastically, "thanks for asking how I am."

"How are you?" I said.

"Better than the raccoon," he said. "It was the size of a *pony*."

N said he'd be right over, and hung up.

I had only been in search of moral support, but this new development pleases me. I have a kind of Malcolm X mentality about triumphing over N: By Whatever Means Necessary.

Yet when he arrives thirty minutes later, he is unscathed. He leans in the doorway, preening in his vintage Danish World War II motorcycle jacket.

No, no, I say to his jacket. To him, I ask, "What is this—your new Single Person wardrobe?"

"I have a right to buy clothes," he says. "It was only ninety dollars at a thrift store."

(*I traded the family cow for it. It came with some magic beans.*)

"Get on with your bad self," I say to him, smiling. "You've become a caricature."

He never wears the jacket again. At least that I know of. Anything is possible.

This is my overall impression of the universe now, a colliding of atoms and no clear direction or purpose at all, except for a growing need for me to get my husband back. His atoms still matter to me. If his atoms cannot be replaced, I swing nimbly in the other direction: I might like to see them rearranged into a bicycle, or a set of fireplace tongs. I feel I have a small nugget of power to incur justice; otherwise I must simply soldier on, my single-mother sleigh heavy with the forty-five-piece set of failed marital luggage I have inherited by proxy.

He kisses the sleeping A, moans, and makes a few nefarious phone calls. (*Whores. Goddamn whores,* I think, oddly placid.) N then attempts to slide out the door. I calmly get in his car, the passenger's seat. My seat.

"You're not leaving," I say. "You're a wreck."

"You can't stop me," he says.

I sit in the seat. He cannot drive away with me. He is momentarily manacled to me. I adore this, and it is so simple. The best things in life always are.

"Just let me make a few phone calls," he says, ". . . then I'll come in to say good-bye. . . ."

"All right," I say, jumping out of the car and flitting inside the house. The ball is in motion, I know he won't leave.

He comes in five minutes later. Throws his keys and wallet on the table and says, "Well, now I *have* to stay."

"Okay," I say. "I'll make up the futon."

He pours himself a large glass of seltzer, ferrets out the last KFC chicken breast, eats it, and says, "Let's go downstairs, where it's warmer.

"I just want to lie down for a minute," he says.

Suddenly he is freezing, shaking, and visibly distraught.

He spends the night. Something he has not done since he left. I sleep better than I have in months. All night I'm constantly aware of him in the house, my senses bristling. All night, I take him in; breathe his scent, a dog of love.

In the morning he's grouchy, as if he's lost at cards. On the interior stairway, he announces that he is going to have a nervous breakdown. This lifts my spirits. He kisses me on the cheek.

I ask, ". . . do you love me?"

Silence.

"How much?" I ask. The old rituals die hard.

"Somewhat," he says.

I have the sense that we have come full circle, back to the beginning of our relationship. The confessions, the groping, the withholding, the wrestling, the protests that amount to nothing. An impression that time will continue to move backwards through this odd second courtship, ticking backwards until he and I are unmarried. The clock hands twirling back to when we have not met, are strangers. In the long run this is a good theory, in light of our pending divorce and the preposterous and irrational actions we're currently undertaking with absolute zeal. So, just perhaps, this is all perfectly formed, like "Circle of Life" in *The Lion King*.

"This will never happen again," he says, emerging from the bathroom fully groomed. His cell phone, its ringer turned off, is apoplectic with missed calls. It is blinking and beeping and virtually jumping up and down. I feel good. I'm kind of *winning*.

"Is there any coffee?" he asks.

"No," I say. "You took the coffee machine."

"Oh," he says.

The next day he brings it back.

So begins a pattern: the Cuisinart toaster. The small armoire. The bed, plus the two nightstands. The large oak entertainment unit. The dining room set and all the Le Creuset. These are all things that technically belong to N, but which he is letting me have in the settlement. The non-Spikenard settlement, the Good Settlement that I am working toward without the hindrance of mercy or scruples. All these objects he has ceded to me, in increments. I am getting rewards for good behavior: I earn this through good conversation, nurturing him through this passage, and submissiveness. Who's using whom? Lines very blurred, rules not plain. But I must say I excel at receiving these prizes, with a genuine thrill. I thank him profusely. I practically *curtsy*.

I suppose it is inevitable that this is going to go on, I rationalize. I just happen to have a child with this man whose presence I cannot do without. It is not a small matter that he also is a gourmet chef, and has a hairy chest but none on his back. Also? I had the best sex of my life on Saturday. I wish I could say this does not matter in the larger scheme of things, but I've always felt that good sex matters a great deal. It is difficult if not impossible to resist being adored, and, perversely, the closer I get to the actual divorce and psychic death, the more enticing this is.

The next day, I tell my mother about this occurrence. Bunny is playing solitaire, and A is playing Twister with himself.

"The amazing thing is," I say sotto voce, *"we're still married."*

Bunny says, "An unfortunate detail, soon to be corrected. Don't let a bit of paperwork drive you to the very brink of delusion. I'd hate to see you become Miss Haversham over this . . . unpleasantness.

"Bastard," Bunny says, slapping down the king of diamonds. *"Bastard."*

I tell Bunny more.

I say, "He's on our futon next to me this morning . . . and we're having coffee . . . and that's when I once again realize we're still married."

"What were you wearing?" Bunny asks, shooting me a look.

"Nothing special," I mumble. "Cutoff Levi's with holes in them. A black T-shirt."

Bunny says, "That's worse than being naked. As you well know. Go on."

"When we hugged good-bye, N reached around and tried to get his hand down the back of my Levi's," I admit. All of this buoys me; if he can still feel any passion for me, all is not lost.

"Is he taking advantage of you?" Bunny asks.

Actually, she says, "He's taking advantage of you."

I am spinning a piece of my hair in my hands. I say to Bunny, "But I liked sleeping with him in the house. How can that be taking advantage? It made me feel loved."

Bunny says, "Exactly."

I ask, "Did you ever sleep with Dad when you guys were in the process of divorce?"

"Constantly," Bunny says. "Best sex of my life. Now can we please drop this? I need to focus."

T-Bone

N came alone to A's birthday party. He quietly and at great length lectured me about accepting Thing Woman, in the fullness of time, while I heartily shucked corn to drown him out. Then he spent the next day, Sunday, grilling T-bone steaks and telling me how fantastic I am and took us all miniature golfing. I am ashamed to be prancing around a windmill in a short denim skirt, flirting with N, to find myself—for this one day—as in love with him as I was when we met. Even the pending divorce we just lightly reminisce over, as though it was a vacation to Fiji, where it rained.

After he left, I just smoked and watched *60 Minutes* and thought, Not a bad life. I gnawed on the leftover T-bones; there is always some meat left.

Nickel

A bit me. He wanted to go outside and get his cardboard space-ship, and I said he couldn't.

I show N the bite. N says, "What can I do to help?"

I say, "I don't know. Move back in? A needs a father around every day, pretty much."

We are at the local mall, in front of the elephant fountain with A. I show my son how to throw some coins in, make a few wishes. A loves the process, the throwing away of money. He has blown through the small change and is grabbing for the quarters. I cut him off. I wish once. I wish for a new washer-dryer. I throw in a nickel, what I feel it's worth, wish-wise. A penny is too little, a dime is too much. Ambiguous on a variety of levels, I still wished the first thing that came into my mind, and that was it.

If only N could stay away. It's seeing him that does it, I think ruefully. I throw in another nickel and wish that.

When he comes back from checking out the new Chinese restaurant in the mall, I stand up and give him a long hug. He is his middleweight, the weight he thinks is fat but his best weight for his face and his form to fit mine. We hug for a long time. We are remembering something.

N says nothing. He was always prudent this way. He has an excellent expression of confusion and pain, which suffices for a no-answer-answer to the unasked question of *What now?*

Abruptly I say, "I don't really want to start over with someone else." I am highly irritated.

N and I enter a pricey children's store where I know we will ridicule the merchandise. God, I miss that. It's the little things, the threads that tie one to marriage. The little things that string together to make one coiled tapestry. N loves to cut, simplify, button up. And the little things fall away, becoming scraps.

To Bunny, I say, "It's like we jumped up in the air and traded places. The girlfriend and I. Except she's not his wife. Now I am the independent unknown woman. It's very Mata Hari. . . ."

"Tick tock," Bunny says. "It was only a matter of time until he swerved. Lovely that it's you, though."

I describe Plan A and B to my mother:

Plan A is to move on and have a good life.

Plan B is to get my husband back.

Obviously I cannot tip my hand to Nadine, my grief counselor, or else she may have me institutionalized or worse, she may stop seeing me. I cannot take another rejection. I am beginning to see why people lie to their intimates. They just can't take it anymore.

Bunny is wondering why I need N back. Still thinking, I watch her face change like a serene sky.

"He's dragging his feet on the final settlement," she notes, pointing a cheese knife at me. "Watch out. You don't actually want him back. Thing Woman would come too."

"Jesus."

I hadn't thought about the practicalities. See, I want things back the way they were, about two years ago, or five. I begin to think about the practicalities of taking back this man. The uncertainty would be massive; it would cover my venue and make A feel like he lived in a bomb shelter. Everyone would just be shuffling cards and eating canned goods, waiting for the next bomb.

Nightmares

Now that I do not want to talk to N, N has the urge to talk to me. It weakens me, of course. Doubtless his intention.

"You know I'll always love you, as a person, Suzanne."

"Yes," I say. "Now go tend to your new life. Have Spikenard make those modifications to the settlement, the ones I gave you last week. Don't forget the cost-of-living increase of 2.5 percent every year. Also, I retain Head of Household tax rights. Go on now."

"Head of Household?" N sallies a protest.

"Yes. That's the parent who doesn't leave," I say. "The one who, in actuality, pays for and does just about everything, while the other parent contributes an obscenely small amount of child support and vacations in Cabo San Lucas."

N calls twice more. Finally, I pick up.

N is whispering and has his hand cupped around his phone receiver: "Don't tell anyone, but I miss A so much. And I *will* always love you. As the mother of my son."

"I know," I say fiercely. "That's why this is so weird. The love won't die."

But the divorce will go through, I understand. I even want it now, although I despise it. I want the prancing ugly legalities done; I grow tired of limbo and acting nice to N all the time so I can keep the microwave or a lawn mower. I want it done, and I intend to essentially triumph in whatever way possible in such a banal, common, and ugly situation where I get dumped like a sack of mealy oats. In this way, I redeem myself as a woman and a force. It's fucked up but true; I am at the gaming board for the duration.

We are, however, able and willing to efficiently exchange psychic wounds over the phone: N has nightmares of something happening to A. He is melting down, like a croque-monsieur.

"I have nightmares about betrayal," I say. "Last night I woke up from a dream saying 'I hate you' into the empty bedroom. Thing Woman is suspended naked from the ceiling, in the dream."

"You spoiled me, I didn't appreciate it. I'm not a good person." N has whispered a non sequitur, his favorite way of avoidance. He is also whispering because he is actually huddled in a food pantry at his house as he speaks to me. Perhaps the cloistered space and the darkness have helped him segue into Confession.

"How could you ever forgive me?" he asks, plaintive. I have no answer. *Pass*.

Then I don't hear from him for a week.

Divorce Police

N returns, presumably from another fantastic sexy luxury resort getaway adventure with his girlfriend. He focuses on the American Beauty rosebush in our yard, which he's laboriously propped back up in a ceremonious fashion. "It's leaning," he says. "Don't just let it die."

"It has spotted-leaf disease, it's sickly, and if it falls over. I'm going to rip it out and replace it," I announce.

"It's still alive. I just didn't do what I needed to do to take care of it," he says.

"Why are you obsessed with the rosebush?" I inquire.

"I miss A. His perfect face," he says. He manages just the right expression of suffering but endurable suffering.

We're outside, someone could hear us. I feel like the house is bugged: the divorce police, making sure everything stays dead.

Later that night, the irony is not lost on me that when I get a call from what my caller ID describes as Caller Unavailable, I *answer it*.

Whenever I call N, he arranges a visitation. Coffee, then wine, then eventually even dinner with A.

When I need him, he comes. We are seeing each other more and talking more than when we were married. Yet I notice I am always glad to see him leave.

N says A is his true family.

Then why is N not here? I know I am at risk.

It's become episodic, my life. This must be the roller coaster all the books describe. But they never say anything about sleeping with the enemy, shopping binges, phone calls at dawn, or finagling for what we single mothers need to survive.

Next day, walking past a Union Street window on my way to the dentist, I see the words BUY ONE, GET ONE FREE on a T-shirt on a storefront mannequin. They are actually dressing these mannequins as I pass. I think about buying one of these marvelous T-shirts and wearing it, that it might be rather sassy.

I remember N saying, lightly and apropos of nothing, after a cocktail party last year, "I can deny anything." He was cocky; he exuded pride, accomplishment, and skill. And what did I say? I said, *OH, MY GOD—THIS WOULD BE THE TIME TO TELL YOU TO LEAVE.* But I didn't say it out loud.

Come on Down!

N and his mother, Françoise, just stopped by for an impromptu visit. Apparently Françoise really wanted a viewing. N called me from down the road to ask if they could both come to pick up A for lunch. I said, "Fine—come on down!"

Five minutes to Françoise, is what I was thinking.

I put on my slim-cut jeans, high-heeled sandals with new French pedicure, dabbed some Coco Chanel behind each ear, applied light foundation and lipstick. I brushed my eyebrows and used a bit of eyebrow pencil, and threw on a fuchsia cashmere sweater and my gold watch. *Ding-dong.*

We kiss in the distant, superficial manner. A shows Françoise all his treasures, while his father, N, walks around all puffed up. The house is uncharacteristically clean and sunny as though for a real estate showing. Françoise gives me a gift and coos over the ambiance, the fresh white tulips (I sent them to myself: a fantastic gambit), and how wonderful I look. She looks good too. Good and curious. She checks inside each closet and room.

This goes on for about thirty minutes and the entire time, N's cell phone is ringing. Ring, ring, ring. By about the fifth call, I say to Françoise brightly, "It's the girlfriend. . . . Short leash."

Françoise just smiles and says, "I don't know. . . ." She knows everything, is the truth, and is just gathering some final data. Meanwhile, N surreptitiously switches his cell phone to vibrate and starts toward my huge stack of unopened mail, his eyes hooded.

I say to Françoise, "Your son is so nosey . . . honey? You don't live here anymore." I place a hand on my mail, gathering it up very casually from his fingers and chuckling as though over a toddler's runny nose. His phone vibrates.

Hummmm. Hummmmm. Hummmmm.

N is, for once, at a loss for words, though I see his eyes squint toward the pile of boxes in the foyer, trying to discern where I was shopping. He opens my refrigerator. N also has data he still needs. He looks like a rooster ready to crow.

Hummmm. Hummmmm. Hummmmm.

N and Françoise both pretend his phone isn't vibrating about two inches from his penis.

As they drive off with A, I stand in the driveway just waving and grinning. Waving and smiling with all my teeth. I feel like royalty. Then I go inside, close the door, and laugh for about a minute.

It was an Academy Award–winning performance. I really found the voice.

In their haste, they drive off without A's shoes. I call N and tell him.

He says, "Oh . . . umm . . . well . . . I'll buy him a new pair."

This has never happened. He has never bought an item of clothing for his son. He is scared as a baby turtle to get back to Thing Woman before the seagulls get him.

"Great!" I say. "A is a size one. Make sure to try them on."

"What? Try them on?"

"Not you, N. A. Let A try them on."

Kneel

N comes to pick up A and he kneels in front of me and weeps. For one crazy moment I think he is going to propose. But instead he talks about how sorry he is.

"How was Mexico?" I ask. He went with Thing Woman.

"Empty," he says with a sad clown expression.

I nod sadly.

Later, on the telephone, Lisa says, "He is full of shit. He's not THAT unhappy. They flew first class, or I'm Dame Elizabeth."

"He always flies first class," I say. I am defending the man who betrayed me and traded me for another woman. A man who could leave a baby boy, his very own son, and subsequently book tickets to Mexico. My knees feel weird.

Lisa says, "He went to Mexico. He climbed *pyramids,* Suzanne."

I consider this and say, "Lisa? I hate your guts, and you're right. But I may not be able to be your friend anymore."

"Call me tomorrow," she says, hanging up.

That night while opening the mail, I receive a charming set of 2.9 percent-fixed-APR checks from my new, open-line credit card company. So I bought:

Entire set of blown-glass fourteenth-century French shoe reproduction Christmas ornaments from the Metropolitan Museum of Art collection

Lace valance and panels for bathroom (Country French Living)

Blond cardigan sweater with detachable white mink collar (Saks)

Vivienne Tam sheer black silk blouse with shoulder cutouts (Saks)

Computer étagère in dark cherrywood (Pottery Barn)

Set of Pottery Barn sheets, duvet cover, and shams—also the matching pashmina throw

Sterling-silver Sphinx bookmark (MoMA collection)

14-karat-gold and ceramic shoe charm bracelet with repro-
ductions of nineteenth-century designer shoes

Earrings to match charm bracelet, in both Royal Blue and
Opera Gold

Italian leather saddle-stitched tote bag (black and maize)

Prelit holiday wreath

I know there are some other things I can't remember. I believe
it came to $4,000. Oh, yes. A Bose Wave CD/radio in platinum
white. The retail purchases and mail order is my fetish, the
opium of the housebound single mother. These purchases have
gotten me through this travesty, box by box. Each box represents
a yard of fog I am attempting to drive through.

When they all arrive, A and I have a Box Party. We open
every box and I'm genuinely surprised and pleased at what's inside. We also eat mint chocolate chip ice cream at this time.

A looks around in wonder and says, "This is all mine, Mommy."
I laugh, something I've been far too unaccustomed to doing, releas-
ing many horny toads from my soul.

Community Service

N is asleep on my couch and I am watching him. I wouldn't mind climbing onto his lap for body heat. It's freezing in this house. No insulation.

The Sawed-Off Madman in my head comments: *As soon as he wakes up, he is running back to Thing Woman, the person he* adores. *You've been a silly slut and have no self-respect whatsoever.*

I am no longer having sex with N. But there is no one in particular that I would rather smell, so there goes the whole Boeing. And I know that in his own slim, irrelevant way, he still loves me.

Christian calls me that night and volleys: "Yes, he loves you in some *sick ass* way, but at what price?"

"The moon," I say. "The galaxy."

Christian says, "What can I do, kitten?"

"Fly up for the weekend," I say. He does. He is there by lunch the following day. We eat thirty dollars' worth of seasonal Dungeness crabs and sing "Indian Sunset" a cappella. It's beautiful. Time stops. We sing "Hit the Road, Jack."

N calls at the very crack of dawn, just as I am coming out of a stupor that involved much dark chocolate from Belgium and a bottle of Kahlúa that danced into White Russians.

"How are you?" he asks.

"I may be dying," I say.

"I'm sorry," he says. His cell phone rings: Thing Woman. "I'll call you back," he says, hanging up. I almost laugh. I see how

Sorry is the two-dollar bill of words. It's worth something, but in the end it's ridiculous, a souvenir at best.

At the beginning of a divorce, a professional-looking woman with red lipstick and horn-rimmed glasses should sit you down with a bottle of Xanax and say, "He will say he still loves you and that he's sorry. By then, it won't matter. You can't believe this now, but you are better off without him." It needs to be a COMMUNITY SERVICE.

At this point, caller ID is my tourniquet and silence is my morphine. Ringer off, volume down on the machine. It's the simple glance system. Access denied.

Bacon

My child support check is late. So I buy a pound of thick-sliced pepper bacon and I wait. Bunny says that men will come if they sense raw meat, especially pork. Sure enough: Ding-*dong*.

"I can't eat," N says. "I can't stay."

But I notice he is shoveling the bacon curls into his mouth. He acts exactly as he always has. His body language says, *I still live here, all this is still mine, and all of you too.*

"N," I ask, "can you ever be happy? Is that possible for you?"

"Yes," he says, riffling through my mail. "I feel fine right now, for example. I feel safe."

We stare at each other, as we used to. Sometimes when we were out at dinner, before A, we would just stare mutely for several minutes at a time, having a conversation with our eyes and eyebrows and lips.

Dat ol' black magik.

"Besides," N continues in his Deepak Chopra voice, which is perfectly true to the live version, "bacon? That is happiness. And if someone is unhappy with some part of their life? It can be corrected. You must truly desire it, though, in its entire beingness."

"I don't want anything," I lie. What I want is a memory-eraser handheld appliance, which I would apply to my forehead. Maybe also a tube sock full of hog manure to slap his face with. My love for A (as well as reality and federal law) prohibits this.

As he goes through the house turning off lights, I can feel him mentally unpacking. Except it is mine now, the house. I feel a taste of strength, power. I don't technically need him. And yet, I need that check.

Bleeder

I've begun to count the days until it's final. The divorce. And yet, I drift.

"I used to be the one you fantasize about," I said to N on the phone, late last night.

"You still are . . . ," N said breezily.

We are not clear on the concept of dissolution. We're being children. It seems to help both of us a great deal.

As for actual content of what N says, I cannot believe him, although I would like to. Trust has scurried under the door of my house, has taken to the street. Yet sentiment stayed behind.

What of my own secret life? Whom did I fantasize about? The truth is that I had stopped. I had become like a scorpion frozen in amber. The best I could imagine was a discontinuation of change.

I said, "I love you."

"I love you too," he said halfheartedly.

"No, I really love you," I said. "Even after everything, I see you and I think, I love your ears. The sound of your voice, your hairline. N," I rasped, "I look at my face sometimes at night and I think, it's a good face. How can you do without this face?"

"It's a wonderful face," he said. "Your skin is flawless."

"I'm so tired," I said. "I find I don't need you, not for survival or grilling food or hauling firewood. But I miss you. I miss having coffee together. I miss your face, rumpled from sleep. I just want you to know that. I love our boy. He looks so much like you."

"He has your bones," he said.

"Yes," I said. "I remember the day he was born."

"It was a beautiful day," he said.

"Everything I have is at least partly because of you."

He protested. "No."

"It is," I said. "The house, A, the writing. Everything. I was born to love you."

"We came from nothing," he said.

Coming from Chicago and San Francisco on full scholarships is not exactly nothing, but we were painting a romantic, bittersweet backdrop here, and we had free creative rein. We were both the first generation in our families to graduate from college. More bonus points from imaginary judges.

I realized we were delivering our eulogy.

"Yes," I said. "Nothing . . . and I do feel nice with you. Just . . . better. That's what it is," I said, thinking: *I don't want to start over with someone new. It's a pain in the ass. You're A's father. I want a real family again.*

Although it is untrue, I imagine we still have a small window of time while I still feel this way. Before I meet someone else. There isn't a queue yet, but one might begin to form at my door any day now and wind around the block, a line of tremendous, emotionally whole men with jobs, hilarious charming self-effacing men with integrity oozing from their demeanor.

Unniversary

I weep on our anniversary as we stand in the bedroom with the door closed, so A won't hear. N cries also; he is crying for himself, for missing his son and his atmospheric, free-radical guilt. On this particular day in the brief history of my life, I am compelled to crush any sign of N's remorse. Remorse is a poor substitute for integrity, surely its natural opposite. One might magnify both remorse and guilt 10000000000000X and end with not one ion of change, positive or negative.

From my place in the first post-split wedding anniversary torture chamber I can see N just a little, like someone standing behind a scrim. I see the fact that N witnessing me come apart is debilitating to his own happiness, stamina, and well-being. A solution? I could be transferred, as one is transferred from one job to a more suitable job, where the climate is more temperate. I could be transferred where I am invisible. I would love this and it is forbidden, along with other fantasies of evasion.

The anniversary date is engraved on several material items of silver and gold and paper, which are now an active malevolence in the house; I have to walk blind, not look at these items directly, and stay to the most basic utensils of the day. I have an intense desire for the twenty-four hours to simply pass, as I wanted the labor pain of our son's birth to pass, to be over. I am birthing a corpse, is the main emotion here.

It is a long day and evening, which essentially blacks me out.

Later that night on the phone, I call him. He answers right away and I say, "I am sorry I was so emotional but . . . that . . . it's just awful. Everything."

"Horrible," he says.

"I just feel as though you don't care about A and me at all."

"That is so untrue."

His cell phone rings in his room and I know it is Thing Woman, of course. My God, the woman has sonar, I think. We both listen to the phone ring.

"Bye for now!" N says, and hangs up the telephone.

Suddenly my place in all this is quite clear. After I hang up, I feel peace. I am not fighting, and I no longer feel I have lost. Everything is right here. Inside. I love him, though he's unworthy and unsuitable and gone completely. That's never going to stop. And I love our son, and so cannot hate him. Our flesh is all mixed together, in A; there will be no unmaking. We may even be together again, in about fifty years. Maybe after the apocalypse.

But why, I think, folding my new sheets fresh from the dryer, *why mess up a perfectly good divorce?*

That night he calls again. But I don't take his call. I want to stick. I want to hold.

Love Child

The next day N comes to pick A up. They drink some chocolate milk and then N takes me aside and leads me into the bedroom of my house. I don't know what he is going to say, but I can see by the black holes of his eyes and the unwavering set of his shoulders that it is not good news for me.

Without preamble, N announces that his girlfriend is pregnant. Eight weeks. They're having it. The news hits me like a blast of warm but potentially dangerous air, pushing me backwards a few steps. I fall on the bed. I think about what this means to their new life, their beginning, N's age (fifty-two), and the fact that he already has one toddler he cannot fully take care of, seemingly. And I do something very unexpected, given my historical preference for tears and pathos: I laugh. I laugh and laugh. I am singing "Love Child" like Diana Ross and laughing hard, clutching my stomach, tossing my hair back. I laugh and dance and sing with quite a bit of verve.

He backs away and leaves the house with A. I am still laughing until I hear the last sound of his car descend the hill, and then I am giggling and saying OH, MY GOD. I fumble for my car keys as though they are an inhaler. I feel there is someone in the room whom I am talking to, presumably my own personal media who want to know how I will incorporate this news. The media wants to know what the lead story is. Hysteria? Homicide? Self-mutilation? Suicide? Accidental Overdose? Epiphany and Resolution via the High Road and a baby gift from Tiffany's for the incoming child?

I drive straight to my mother's house. On the way, I stop tittering and the horror sinks in.

I stand in my parents' living room and, in a crackly wry voice, announce this new development. She is dusting.

"These men are busy busy busy," Bunny says. "It's another slap," she acknowledges, putting down a ceramic elephant a bit harder than necessary. She rummages in her purse for a minute.

"I am okay, I will be okay," I rasp. "But the anguish and the jealousy on A's and my behalf is just massive and leery. It's like a big black hole that is sucking my whole heart down its maw."

"I think that sounds perfectly normal right now," Bunny replies. "Of course you're in shock," she says.

For a while now, I haven't truly wanted him back, not in a real-life, tangible sense. I just wanted to win. Yes, I wanted A to have his father back. But even more than that, if I am perfectly honest with myself, I wanted to win my husband back. I needed it more.

Perhaps, a thin, reedy voice in my heart says, *you have won by losing.*

IV
Grief

We know desire nothing can relieve.

—Mephistopheles

Never Is Here

The flip side of love is disregard. When entering the country of a certain kind of love, be aware that desolation is a distinct possibility. I had no such singular hindsight. I've had time, however, and my focus has improved, my eyes have sharpened. Now when I look back, it's all there in impeccable array, like Orion.

I intend truth, but some of what I believe to be true is doubtless untrue. Due to necessity, I will aim for the broad strokes. The loss of significant chunks of highly salient information, the blurring of whole months is a wily, elastic aspect of betrayal. When lovers warp truth, there will be no full straightening at any subsequent hour. I occasionally find myself sitting in a quiet room with A, smoothing out the missing pieces of my married life with N, scrutinizing time and events with absent fingers, as I mold Play-Doh elephants and read Dr. Seuss to him.

I don't think even N knows all of what happened. He forgets things, N does, one would imagine deliberately, and then they're gone. He doesn't know the date of my birthday, A's birthday, or his own family's birthday. He goes blank. Not in important conferences, of course; not on the scheduled maintenance on his motorcycle. He remembers what's important to him; we all do. When we were married I took on a supportive yet essential role: I Am N's Memory. I was the wife remembering the times and the dates of all events, and when the cards and the recycling and the invitations should go out; I actively and efficiently trafficked the requirements of the everyday. I considered this the normal duty of a wife, perhaps even a privilege. I felt proud and well rewarded simply to serve in silence, like a Saint Bernard carrying a small keg under its chin.

In a just universe, there would be a place where love and marriages go to die, rapture's own version of the elephants' graveyard. They should not be allowed to dissipate on their own, to float away on some random moment, irrevocable as seed from a dandelion. There ought to be a body you can bury. A gravesite: Here Lies the Marriage of N and S, with beginning and ending dates inscribed into the marble. One could visit the grave, say a few words. Instead I am faced with an acidic sense of loss and the feeling that a passage has been missed in the scheme of things. There are so many marriage ceremonies, there ought to be one for divorce. Instead of rice, people could throw fistfuls of cash and light hallucinogens.

I also wish I could send a message into every tortured, depressed, and betrayed woman's mind at this very moment so they would just turn mid-step and say with perfect clarity to their husbands:

"Oh, wait—this is crazy. I'm leaving you. Feel free to go and make some other lucky woman's life into this exact shade of black."

Signing

N and I sign the final divorce settlement papers. It is a Saturday, so there's no day care and A is with us. This should be illegal but it isn't. You have to kill someone to get any attention. I feel a sudden kinship with killers . . . killers and widows. I have a friend who is a widow. I take a moment to envy her.

A runs around the floor playing with brochures and Tic Tacs. Tic Tacs are all we have. Then A wanders off, and for a terrible moment I think he's gone into the street, because the door to the notary office is propped open.

A, it turns out, has wandered into a small side office; he wanders out. N and I grip the counter as the notary checks our driver's licenses. Then she asks a few basic questions. She is expressionless. Her name is Juana; a man sits at a desk writing something and doesn't look up. Lucifer, probably. Quietly logging us in.

Three days later I call N.

"When are the waves of relief going to begin?" I ask. He doesn't answer.

Day four and Christian calls every day at noon, as though I am on suicide watch. I keep picking up old conversations wherever I've left them, to whoever is in my kitchen or electronic air space.

"Hey you," Christian says. It's 12:01 p.m.

"I've worn out everyone I know. I can't call anyone because they are all used," I say to Christian as I clean my refrigerator with a toothbrush and Comet. I don't say hello.

Christian says, "I know, baby. Just talk to me. I'm listening." I can tell by the whimsical list of his voice that he's back into his porn, he's surreptitiously examining the *Los Angeles Times* travel section.

"Morocco is so over," Christian says. "So you're still alive?"

"Most of me."

"Has there been new movement?"

"In a way. It finally hit me that N is neither exceptionally kind nor honest nor compassionate, and it just slays me. I was bonded to him, and so now I feel like an amputee and a fool, Christian. To be wrong about the most basic attributes of my mate stuns me. To realize I am a zebra and he is a lion. Those two animals *can't live together*. And yet there is A. So there must be a blueprint of some kind."

"Everything is going according to plan," Christian says. "Just not the plan you made."

"One day I hate his guts and the next day I'm trying to be reasonable and even friendly. One day I'm crying at beer commercials, and the next I'm on the phone to my agent making jokes about how much better my career and life are going without him. One night I let him tuck A in, the next he walks in and I say, *Hello, Rasputin*. And everywhere, everyone tells me to Let Go, but they don't tell me *how*. I'm flailing. I have good days and bad, Cinderella and Sea Witch.

"I didn't have a plan for this," I say. A lightbulb flickers in the kitchen. It's another sign. "But I can make a plan, based on what I know now."

"Okay. Of course you can. I can't believe the deals they have on London," Christian says.

(Click.)

Egg

Today I wake at five a.m. and I cannot believe my first thought is, I miss N. The way he brought coffee, sometimes an egg. His early assessment of the newspaper. My second thought is that N is having a baby with Thing Woman. And so I brush it all away, get up, and have a cigarette and coffee with half-and-half and check my e-mail and take a shower and it's still there. If anything, it is heightened by my instant repression. The egg and the coffee seem omnipotent to me now, a secret ritual I will be forever banned from, due to my own divorce crimes.

Grief, which has hovered all along on my periphery, occasionally wholly engulfs me. Lately you may see me crying in a public place for no apparent reason. I snap back rather quickly. My immune system seems capable. And there is still a slim frond of pride. As I browse through the Mill Valley shops, I keep a casual, interested, and serene mask in place, so no one I know will be able to say they saw me and I looked Devastated.

It will pass, I know from experience. And, more and more over the months, it feels pure. More a simple feeling, a sweet or sour memory that hums in tandem with the ambient sounds of my life, and considerably less a call to action. Nothing can be done, I know. That desired, mutually conceived baby of theirs is coming. They're coming, three of them, now—and we're going. We're just two leftover. That's the net. I used to struggle and keen and bargain, but now I just hunker down into the recess. Without much ado, I see it's just as Kerouac said: *Accept loss forever*.

I feel as if the reel on the movie of my life has simply snapped and I've been sitting in the dark theater for some time. My mother holds firm.

"He's GONE. He's off the deep end. But you can't attend him. You can't be the ex wife that's never quite the ex."

"I know," I say.

"But it's tricky, because he's A's father. He's the father of the future king, so it's a Diana thing in reverse. You just know Charles wanted to bash her bulimic head in with a cast-iron skillet, but she was the mother of the future kings. You have to think about how he matters to A, and guard that," Bunny orates from my kitchen.

I do know all this. I build N up to A; I insulate his grief and loss. It is because of A, but I've discovered after many failed experiments that it is also a natural paradox: In much different ways, I have to love them both. Loving one or the other is impossible.

N doesn't deserve fealty, but this is irrelevant. Whoever deserved what they received? I will swallow the grief so N doesn't.

The grief is bitter and seeps out in a black trickle from the woman in me, temporarily rendering me depleted, crooked. The woman takes it all in daily, lets it pass, finds out it isn't crippling; the mother in me gives and receives what I can grasp at hand.

The woman and the mother, and not in that order. It has to be mother first, A first, thus these two bright puppets I flail around the stage of our new life, just A and me. I try to make it seem as though N is almost there, or has just stepped out for a cigar. His wonderful daddy who loves him so much has stepped out for a long cigar. My former companion has stepped out.

"He is A's only father," Bunny says with a great sigh, almost a snort. "You have to give in gracefully, but only when A is around. The rest of the time, it doesn't matter what you think or say. It surely doesn't matter to him. He's a shape-shifter. Shape-shifter, leaving behind a perpetual line of deserted snake skins . . ." She is peeling an apple in one long red swirl. ". . . Each bigger than the last."

"I know."

What I know is not pretty, but it is knowledge nonetheless. Grief, I understand with icy clarity, is simply information I allow myself to know.

Yet life spins onward. In happier news, I learn that in his very own garage in Beverly Hills, Christian wraps himself up as a present for his new girlfriend on her birthday: a bow on his head, ribbon around his penis.

"Naturally she saw through it as the cheap disguise it was," he says to me on the phone later that night.

He forgot, in other words. Christian has not remembered

anything in his life, a killing trait that once again he manages to pull off with a minimum of real trouble from anyone in authority.

"I like to mix it up," Christian says. "I may marry her; she laughed. And she didn't wait for me to give her something else, some godforsaken watch or something from Cartier. She just went on naturally."

I think for a moment. I say, "I like her. I can just tell. I can tell from here."

I tell Christian I'm very happy for him, and that I may never remarry.

Christian says, "Oh, I don't believe that. I know the real Suzanne. Who you are."

"Who am I?" I ask him. "I know I'm not the girl on the campus lawn with you in 1985, and I know I'm not the woman who got married and I'm not the woman I was before childbirth. But who am I now?" I ask.

He doesn't really answer. As if to say, You know and I know and don't ask stupid questions. As though answering would break a spell, a rule of our secret contract.

Abruptly, Christian says, "You know that overwhelming feeling of love you have for A?"

I wait.

"That's what it will be like," Christian says.

It's very heartbreaking and kind. I feel that my core people are firmly nudging me past grief and, once again, toward the flower-strewn arena and soon I'll see a naked bull pawing the ground and it'll be like "You again." If I'm *lucky*.

Hemlock

Good things spring up. A nice bone of a magazine job lands in my territory. I also have my own personal graveyard. I see N twice a week. He walks among us, a ghost. When we hug it's like hugging no one. Gone. Vertical corpse.

The bone thrown my way is this: I have become the columnist for a national women's magazine, in addition to my other free-lance work. The editor in chief said she had read and liked an essay I published, and their monthly columnist was moving on.

It came out of the stark atmosphere, this career opportunity. My heart is still broken, one eye still black. One event doesn't make up for the other, but it helps, and I know two things: More good career waves will come, now that I don't care. And I know N is emotional hemlock, and do my best to not eat him.

"Eat Kentucky Fried Chicken once a week," says Nadine at our next session. "Buy the four-piece dinner meal value pack, with extra coleslaw. And cry when you need to. Do not attempt to hold it back . . . left to fester, it could become brackish."

STUG

Nadine introduces me to STUG: Sudden Temporary Upsurge of Grief.

I *love* STUG. She also promotes me to the fourth stage of my healing: reinvestment in self.

"N is a catalyst for your healing," she tells me. "He's forcing you to move on. But the more you allow yourself to be available to him, the more he will erode your sense of self."

"Why?" I ask, belligerent. I feel really normal, a privileged and legal loose cannon now that I know about STUG, as if I've bought duty-free on a plane.

Nadine says, "Every time you ask Why. Especially every time you ask N Why. You're hooked. You are not in your power.

"There is a stock answer," she says, leaning forward as if in a high wind. "He is not compassionate. He missed the empathy classes. His only bedside manner was fucking you."

I gasp.

Then I say, "Oh, my God. You're right."

I blow my nose.

"The dilemma is such that if I see him and he's nice, I feel bad—and if I see him and he's nasty, I also feel bad," I whine. "The answer is not to see him. Yet with a child in common, I must see him, unless I manage to go blind in some ancient Grecian medical emergency."

"Use this time to wrap your mind around his abandonment," Nadine says, firm.

"Right. A little something in a grief turban."

Nothing from Nadine. An infinitesimal nod, just. She doesn't do take-backs.

"You know what I believe? I believe this is all random bad luck, which is suffusing the planet. I chose the wrong surprise prize bag. Yet there is an evening-out phenomena also: This may be why God recently created vodka in all new flavors."

Nadine doesn't move a hair. She refuses to dance. She instructs me to make a list of Pathological Awareness. I'm also to contact a woman named Hyacinth to inform me of the karmic implications of this union. Then, Nadine implies, I may begin to approach the roots of truth and thereby, peace.

I ask Nadine: "Is there a there, and if so, when do I get there?"

"Now," Nadine says.

Naturally, I want to do all this my way: The slow, balled-up way with instant gratification and circular patterns I can negotiate blindfolded. But I can't, because Nadine is a witch and will know.

Dream Wedding

I have a dream about my wedding. A dream that time-travels back to my wedding, with shaky cam. And I'm at the minister kissing N when I see that there is an empty chair right in the front row. An empty chair, and every other chair filled, and then I look away at N. We are about to head down the aisle as everyone stands to see the bride and groom. And it is then I see that Thing Woman is sitting in that chair, grinning like a tiger.

They go off together in a black car, Thing Woman and N, and one by one the party dissipates until I'm alone. From a distance, A comes down the path toward me and I feel glad, but I'm still looking where their car disappeared, I can see it, a speck. A is wearing a tiny tuxedo and says, "I will take you home, Mommy."

"No," I moan when I wake up. "No."

Later, A and I are listening to Pablo Casals and playing. A is building a time machine and the sun is slanting into my eyes so the eyelashes go all starry and I remember the whole dream, and my eyes fill. A plays Time Machine; he builds the ship around my prone body, which is stretched on the carpet.

"Where are we now?" I ask.

"Dinosaur time."

"But we'll be eaten."

"No, I have missiles."

"Oh, good. Thank you, Captain A."

"I'm not the captain, remember, Mommy? You're the captain."

"Right." I cover my eyes, ostensibly to deflect the enemy fire.

"Now we use the camouflage . . . ," A says.

"I love the camouflage," I enthuse. I would like to stay here forever.

"Uh-oh," A says. "We can't go back in time."

"Why not?"

"Because the missiles aren't working and the . . ."

"I want to go home now," I say.

"We can't, Mommy."

Oh, yeah, I think, pulling A's hand to hold.

When N comes the next day, I hand A off at the door, don't see his face. At the supermarket, they proffer half-dollar-sized cupcakes laden with an inch and a half of that spectacular lardy frosting, with multicolored sprinkles, no less. Eighteen to a package—half chocolate with white icing, half the reverse. As I tip them into my cart, I rationalize that they will be a treat for A, something innocuous yet rewarding. We will form small bonding ceremonies around each one. I eat five this night. They are right now murmuring to me from the kitchen:

Listen. One more can't hurt. We're tiny. Really. No worse than oxygen.

"You can't run and you can't hide," A says just before bed, apropos of nothing.

Daddy's Water

N picks A up. I can't seem to stop from sneaky and silent crying, sometimes, when I see him now. I don't know why; it might be because he has taken to wearing the same Mr. Science glasses he was wearing at the hospital when A was born. I used to hate those glasses. Now I want them bronzed. I want them away from where he can wear them without me.

They come back. I cry and make no sound, so A won't hear. But he does, in that scary way children have. He comes over and says, "Mommy?"

"Mommy has a cold," I say.

"I love you, Mommy."

"I love you too," I say.

"Let it go," N hisses, seeing my wet face.

Yes. But how? After N leaves, A goes to his water glass on the coffee table.

"This is Daddy's water," he says.

"Yes," I say. A sticks in a straw and makes bubbles in it. I remember doing that, how my parents always told me to stop. Make bubbles, I think. Make all the bubbles you want, my man.

A places the glass reverently back in the same spot. "This is Daddy's water," he says again.

"Yes," I say.

He brings it to me. He makes his mother drink. I drink. Some kind of communion is taking place. I understand little, A understands all.

Oxygen

N calls from his cell phone. We have a poor connection.

"Can you hear me?" he says.

"Yes," I say, after a full minute. Not answering is powerful. Just let the oxygen collect. Commit to nothing. Be nothing.

"I wish I were dead," I tell him.

"I'm so sorry," he says.

"No, you're not."

"Yes, I am."

"I feel like I'm not even a woman anymore," I say. I hang up.

Night. A stretch limousine picks me up to spirit me to the airport, to the television talk show where they will air my humorous B segment, based on the single-mother monthly column I write. I am in Los Angeles. I ride in the huge black-leather upholstery. There is only me.

I call N back. I describe the limo, how there is a bar and a DVD and television.

"I wish you were here," I say. The words fly embarrassed out of my mouth, like spittle.

From the window of the limousine I'm watching trains go in the opposite direction. There is no one inside the trains; I don't know why. The trains seem ineffably sad. Their sound soothes me, however. I am feeling many things at once.

Talk Show

I knew I was in trouble when I arrived at the studio and they said, "The Divorce Lady is here." Not the monthly column writer. The Divorce Lady.

I go through makeup and hair. The woman straightens my hair with a flattening rod.

My hair is not flat enough. They do it all again. There, she says. I smell my scalp burning. *Good,* I think. *Good.*

I am attached to a mike.

I think: *I am the humorist who writes the column in the glossy women's magazine, which the producer read and thought would make a good B segment to the real show. I of course agreed. Now I am sure I was mistaken. Now that the cameras are rolling, rolling, rolling.*

When the video segment that was previously taped comes onto the screen above the stage, I watch, marveling at how nice my tiny house looks, at how thin my eyebrows are. How who I think I am is so different from who I really am. How one eye is larger than the other, like Marty Feldman. Only my teeth look right. I focus on teeth.

As a camera swivels toward me like a cannon, I watch myself on the screened segment, moving around my own home—pretending to make tea, pretending to write on a laptop. Pretending to make fun of myself, to be a wry seasoned divorced woman. As I sit and watch, I am pretending to enjoy it. Then suddenly there is my wedding video. They have decided to use part of that too. I see myself walking down the aisle, looking sideways. I gasp, but not aloud. My heart gasps.

There is something different about this woman, this bride who was I. She is happy. She seems about twenty years younger, instead of eight years younger. Then I see N in his white tuxedo jacket, smiling brightly at me as I approach him in my wedding dress, and I freeze. I see us kissing at the altar. I can't believe they have chosen to air this as part of my B Segment Lifestyle Video Collage. Also, it is Valentine's Day now. The irony seems a fist. A fist in my eye.

I smile and look interested. I try not to scream the word *No*.

At the end, the host thanks the audience. Then she leaves the studio. I smile and applaud her back. There is nothing else to be done. I have no power here. I am The Divorce Lady. They tell me how well I've done, how funny I was. I thank them. I am escorted to the back door, where a car waits to take me away.

On the airplane going home, I want so much to tell the woman next to me that my ex husband left. That this is my first

Valentine's Day since the divorce. The woman is next to her husband; clearly they have been married for decades. She is knitting a blue baby blanket. *We had a boy too,* I want to say. I stop just short of actually doing this. Instead, I jam a tiny wine bottle in my mouth.

For the first time in my life, I feel truly spent. And uncertain of the future, which seems to be a door with a dark shadow, and then nothing. I myself am casting the shadow. I'm afraid of the door.

And the Sawed-Off Madman says, *You can't cry just for being sad anymore. Haven't you read the newspapers? Are you confused about the rules? You're a single mother now: One income in the priciest place on the globe. And now you're eight hundred times more likely to file for bankruptcy, because you're a single mother. Dig it. Yeah, babe! Be glad for a roof and heat. Be glad we haven't thrown you out on your* face.

Damage Control

I observe that the unlooked-for goodness of the lost husband (in that all lost husbands are axiomatically bad) is that you have once and for all achieved damage control: They can no longer deliberately spill ashes on the carpet, threaten you with legal decimation, or get lost in the spiky Italian alps rather than look at the map. Further examples abound: A sees N thrice a month for pure unadulterated father-son time. A does not daily witness his abrupt fits of pique—interspersed, as I recall from A's infancy, by periods of zombie checked-out behavior and general neglect. A doesn't wake to see his parents argue or his mother weeping hysterically. Yes, it is good to look at everything from all sides. I feel I am becoming wide-screen.

Physically I am badly near-sighted, needing glasses not for reading but for everything else. So I leave my glasses off when N visits A. I can hear him dancing and prancing in his new happy life scene from *Showboat*, but I can't see him. I even ask a couple of questions and remain neutral and it still works. Genius.

"If you're upset and you're in front of your children, don't look into their eyes," I write in my single-mother column: "Think vampire."

Not so absurd a comparison, at this point in time. After all, he has divorced me. What can I get from him emotionally now that would mitigate that insulting legal quagmire? The quicksand is already up to my waist. Best not to struggle, to take the path of least resistance, as usual, the Sufi mind-set is impeccable.

I think about how a vampire drains his victim just to the brink of death but keeps her alive. This is akin to what N did the last year of our marriage, perhaps longer. And I swooned just like those 1920s actresses in filmy white low-cut negligees. I invited him into my bedroom, too. I had not been spoken to, I had not been warned.

I regret how few speak for all of the leeched wives and their children, left behind for all new families. Few enough provide support, or simply the courage to jump, to those standing on the edge of a precipice. To jump despite the great fear.

We are often pushed, I reflect.

Yet I look in the mirror and I see less fear, not more.

It may be what Annie Lennox refers to as "the call of the living." I have to listen hard for it. It's important to know I am still perfectly human; I have been divorced yet remain lovable and capable and I must teach A all this by example, the most vital task of all.

Divorce: From Parker Brothers!

Bunny and I are inventing a new board game, based on divorce. She is in my house and she brought pork buns from The Slanted Door, a reason to live if I ever tasted one. She leans over my kitchen table, leering down at the board like Michael Douglas in *Wall Street*.

"Greed is good," Bunny says.

"Greed is healthy," I assert. "It may be the only form of revenge available to the abandoned women and single mothers of America."

"Hell, yes," Bunny agrees happily, knocking back a scotch.

We have all the spaces on the board mapped out. Instead of choosing a little metal shoe or a race car or a dog for your own playing piece, like in Monopoly, you get to choose from a heart, a tiny lead anvil, a bag of money with wings, a headless woman, a skillet, or a gun. You can play as many times as you want. No one wins. It is a circle-shaped board with the following squares to traverse before you get to the finish line, and then the circle begins again:

Infatuation
Joy
Pressure
Marriage
Honeymoon
Parties
Weekends away
Domestication
Baby
Conflict over childcare
Neglect of wife
Belligerence
Depression
Paranoia
Beginnings of the *I'm not Happy* speech
Infidelity
Trying to save marriage
Hopelessness
Panic
Gaslight torture time: husband denies everything
Ineffectual marriage counseling
More panic
The walkout

Shock
Single parenthood
Denial
Trying to make it okay
The Outing of the mistress
Rage/Fuck everyone
Resignation
Divorce
Financial chaos
Bitterness
Grief
Surviving
Contentment
Joy

Classic Memory

My husband, N, came in the bedroom very worried because he had received a letter from a collection agency in San Jose. A medical bill he knew nothing about, for $297. He showed it to me, hoping I can change its meaning.

I have a perfect credit record, he said.

He wandered room to room with the letter in his hand, tight-lipped. As though he were escorting police through the house.

Once again, I resisted the urge to laugh.

It occurs to me now that maybe a marriage where you are not allowed to laugh is not worth fighting for. I think of how I gave myself up to control the outcome.

Alone in that same house now and at peace, I realize that pride makes us think we control our destiny and the people we love. Pride and naïveté, the twin set of the unconsciousness.

However, I notice I also recall how beautiful he looked as he walked through our domicile. I know he was playing to me, his audience; he made it seem charming and humorous. A moment.

Emerald City

A has a Winnie the Pooh doctor's kit, a stethoscope and a fake needle/shot.

And we are on the beanbag chair (denim, bought secondhand from summer camp) in his room. A is with me, we are comfortable and free.

And so I feel brave and I say, "Would you like to check my heart, Dr. A?"

"Yes," he says. "Wait."

Then he puts on Burger King 3-D glasses and his stethoscope, and we put it on my heart to listen.

"How is my heart?" I ask.

"Not good," A says with a matter-of-fact demeanor.

I burst out laughing. A remains serious.

"Well, what should I do?" I ask.

A tells me that I have too much water on my heart.

"So what should I do to make my heart better?"

"You should sleep, and then the water on your heart will go away," he says.

"Ahh. Thank you, Dr. A."

A then reaches over to get his purple plastic fake needle; without preamble, he gives me a shot in the arm.

"Was that for my heart?"

"Yes," A says.

"Thank you."

Later he gives me several of his treasures to examine. I pick out the $1.98 magic wand from Fairyland in Oakland. My son is still dressed as Dr A.

"Would you like to cast a spell on me?" I ask.

"Yes," A says, waving the wand back and forth, using vigorous motions. "You'll be better tomorrow," he announces.

"Oh, good. Brilliant. I really appreciate this."

Oh, I love him, I think. There is nothing I wouldn't do for him. Nothing. Therein lies the difference between N and me, the difference that can never be overcome: putting himself over his son, not to mention his wife, whom he knew was true and had loved him despite all the myriad maladies of his soul. Now A is Guest Son and not Whole Son status, a marginalization, rife with so many subtle mind-fuckings to the both of them. I hope not. Yet nothing can ever change what happened to them, or my part in it. It's too late for regret or change and it was the moment he climbed up on the manic dolphin and swept away from us, toward his own private Atlantis.

Despite these higher gropings at insight and what can be found as positive, I am still on a first-name basis with Jesus, because when the pain gets unbearable, I say under my breath, *Jesus, walk with me. Walk with me, Jesus. Take this pain, I can't take it. It's too big for me.* When we are traveling alone and suddenly A says, apropos of nothing, "Bye-bye, Duh Duh!" I'm holding on to my very last dime of faith and sanity. *Jesus,* I say. *Come in, Jesus*.

Jesus sends Lisa instead. She stops by in a crocheted dress, with an armful of snapdragons, and tells me exactly what to do.

". . . replace all the sheets. Hotel quality will do. Take daily warm, deep baths with lavender and rosemary scents. Also have a full and not 'express' manicure/pedicure without delay. You want the color to be pale beige. Yes . . . pale beige for mourning, and not a frost, a matte. Naps of long and vulgar lengths should also be rigorously taken. If you think I'm not serious, Suzanne, you are deeply mistaken. This is the very best of what I know about attending to loss, which is a lot," Lisa concludes.

I say, "Also? I'm dead afraid of getting involved with another man. Call me a fool, but I can't sustain any more loss for quite some time. It is not even clear that I have sustained this loss."

"BUT. You know you're going to have another relationship, right?" Lisa says.

"I'm afraid so," I say.

"That's exactly right," Lisa says.

"But not yet. I'm not even close to ready," I say.

This is known as the Hell No We Won't Go School of Dating. We've talked of this many times; I have vehemently denied any future interaction with the opposite sex. I stress that, like, they're opposite for a *reason*. But now that N's been gone almost a year, and I've seen every *Seinfeld* episode four times, I am beginning to come to the horrible conclusion that I may have to start all over with someone else.

And it's so awful and yet so hilarious, if I think about it for even a minute. 'Cuz while I wuz making all those plans, laying all those plans so carefully, ordering wedding invitations and birth announcements and Scandinavian design armoires—God one day looks down and says, *Oh, dear. How did THAT get over THERE???* And He reaches down and rearranges everything, "redirects" a few marriages. Mine included.

Sunday, and my mother takes me to lunch at Denny's. We are right in the middle of our sandwiches when she casually asks: "Do you think you'll get married again?"

And I know she wants me to, though Bunny would have her ears pulled off before she'd admit to it. Given her 230-year marriage to Ron, Bunny refuses to see the truth about marriage, which is that it is not safe; again and again I've assured my mother that marriage would not flourish as an amusement park ride. Right now, the base stupidity of the question seems astonishing: *Do you think you'll try lion taming again? Only this time you'll be so much wiser—knowing everything you've learned. Don't you want to lion tame again? With that one good arm?*

"I don't want that," I say in a hollow voice. I'm looking out the plate-glass window of the restaurant as though a medieval execution is setting up outside. French villagers capering about a guillotine. I feel removed, observing myself, and part of me is stepping to the side to let this huge thing by. This bone-clattering grief mobile, this carriage of divorce.

"I don't want to center my life around a man," I say woodenly. It is the truth, but it is also a cliché, and therefore sounds like tripe.

"I don't think anyone should get married unless they want children. . . ."

I hear myself saying this even though it is possibly the most cynical remark ever made, one I heard from Christian before my own marriage was celebrated. At the time, I was aghast. Now I just feel old and embittered, though a slim part of me hopes I am wrong.

Emergency Grief Squad

I am sifting through A's infant toys to clear space out of my window boxes for his new toys. Two of the window boxes hold baby toys, and one of them holds photographs. I am not going near the photographs, but then I see myself, as on close-circuit camera, reaching out and lifting the long rectangular white wooden top off the third window box. I am drawn toward this third box, not fully realizing that it is stuffed with Kryptonite. Once I see the first bag of pictures, I sense the Kryptonite, but I rationalize my next act.

Kryptonite renders Superman powerless, and this is why I want to banish this box of Kryptonite from my living room area. It's a beautiful day and I am sure I can accomplish this one small task. Surely I can handle doing a pass through the pictures and separating out the ones that are deadly to look at.

Within minutes, I pluck out of the bag a single photograph of N. He is holding a shopping bag with silk sunflowers in it, in the small quaint town of Calistoga. His face, his entire demeanor, emanates a most intense yet gentle love and servitude. I am taking the picture. It is the mid-nineties and I have no idea what the future holds. I hold the photograph at arm's length and I look at the expression on his face and I choke, as though a giant marshmallow is stuck in my throat. I am seeing a ghost, yet a person who is still alive and available in this fashion to someone else.

I realize he hasn't looked at me this way in years. And the impossibility of getting that look back or living without that man who holds the bag of silk sunflowers, the father of my child, hits me full in the chest and I begin to hyperventilate. I clutch the rest of the pictures and toss them into a large Macy's bag and I sit in the middle of the rug and I howl. The phone is ringing. It's Lisa. I pull myself together in the remarkable way of imposters and insane people, single mothers in particular.

"Hello?" I lilt.

"It's Lisa," she says.

I am breathing hard, fighting for control and that telephone voice I need to get through this and off the phone without Lisa calling the paramedics.

"SUZANNE. WHAT'S WRONG?"

I am breathing in and out, in and out, and saying something to the effect of "SAD . . . SO SAD . . . REALLY SAD. I CAN'T BELIEVE THIS, YOU HAVE TO SEE THIS. . . ."

"Should I come over?"

"YES."

I hold my hand to my mouth. The gods have seen fit to have my front lower tooth crown pop off. I hold it in my hand. It's cracked. I can't glue it back on. I put it in an empty sugar dish. I look in the mirror. My face is slick with tears, my hair is stuck to my head with sweat, and I am missing a front tooth. I look like a witch that they tried to drown but who popped back up in Boston Common. I look medieval. And just exactly like a sad crazy ugly witch. It's perfect. And my dentist is in Italy. I will be toothless for at least a week. I feel actively glad. Finally things are starting to match up.

"GIVE ME TWENTY MINUTES. I NEED TO GET SOME CAKE," Lisa says, and hangs up.

"Thank you," I say to the dead phone. And I sit on the rug and I rock and I wait. I try not to pick up any more photographs; I leave everything just as it is. Lisa is going to have to take care of this. I mentally see A at my parents' house, running and playing. I am so glad he isn't here. He shouldn't see his mother with the Kryptonite; I am like a Superman to A and he cannot see me this destroyed.

Lisa arrives bearing three kinds of cake. Lemon cake, coconut cake, and chocolate cake. She prepares tea and sets it before me on the ottoman near the window boxes.

I hold the sunflowers and N's picture to her face and I say, "LOOK AT THIS."

She examines it, as though looking at a crime photo. She closes her eyes. Palms the picture.

"I know," she says softly.

"LOOK!" I say, grabbing it away from her and holding it high in the air. Its terrible glossy finish glistens in the light.

"WHO IS THIS? WHO IS THIS?" I demand, sobbing and slapping my hand on my thigh.

"It's him," she says. "It's him before."

"I NEED HIM BACK," I say. "I CAN'T STAND THIS."

"I know, honey. I know." Lisa hugs me. She doesn't say anything about the fact that I am missing a front crown.

"It's going to be all right, I promise," Lisa says.

"OH, LISA," I say.

"OH, HONEY," she says, holding me so tight, I can smell her hair. She smells like freedom, like someone who is free. She helps me throw all the photos into the bag to put away in the store-room.

I can't eat cake, but I drink some tea.

She never says anything about my missing tooth. She sees it as the meaningless detail it is. She also knows that to talk about the tooth would be to miss the entire point.

We throw the bag of pictures over the deck and it lands near the storeroom. Lisa goes down and transfers the bag into the storeroom. She leaves the cake and sits with me for a long time while we say nothing. Soon I fall asleep and when I wake up, Lisa is still here, reading *Real Simple* magazine and drinking Pepsi from a red wineglass. Extra ice.

"Cake?" she says.

"Please," I say.

We eat the cake with a bottle of Beaujolais nouveau. Something has been accomplished, something very hard and vital and necessary, which I needed Lisa for. She is the emergency grief squad, roaring to my curb in the right time and place, saving me, and, not to mention A, by proxy.

Control

I ask Nadine why it is taking me so long to get free of N.

"Repetition compulsion," Nadine says, adding, "if you want the fancy term for it."

I see it was often me baiting that hook, throwing emotional logs into blazing debates and passionate revenges. *The role of Wicked Embittered Shrew was played by Suzanne Finnamore.* And there were other roles I embraced. When he would call, I would say, *Have you been thinking about us?* Or, *Do you miss us?* Or I would start very deliberately emoting in the direction of *Lost Without You.*

"Okay, but, Nadine . . . ," I say. "I mean, look at me. I'm a smart woman; I'm not entirely masochistic. But when he left, I kept going back to that river. Why did I do this?"

Nadine immediately delivers one long and apparently well-thought-out sentence.

"If I put you into a five-hundred-gallon drum and sealed it up, and had a helicopter brought in to swing it over a raging gully, I know what you would want."

She extends one finger in my direction.

"Control," Nadine says, leaning back in her chair and rubbing her hands together.

"Opium?" I suggest, as if Nadine hadn't answered. "A cookie?" I ask.

Nadine does not flinch. "Opium and cookies would be the substitute for the control," she says.

"What if I still love him?" I say. This is the joker in this deck of personal growth and sensible analysis. I know now that Nadine will try to talk me out of loving N. But she doesn't.

"It's okay to love him, as long as you stay clear on who he is," Nadine says.

"A lover without borders," I murmur. "A man without boundaries. A good man, but not for me to be married to. And the father of my son."

"There you go," Nadine says. "There you are."

Ashes

I fall asleep very late, reading about the *Titanic, A Night to Remember*. I bolt awake at three a.m., steeped in blackest ennui. And the Sawed-Off Madman started slowly but surely having a field day in my brain. He was having a huge bash, champagne corks popping in his glee. He said, *RIGHT ON, YOU ARE FUCKED*. He wanted me to take a couple sleeping pills, drink some wine, smoke some pot, he wanted it all. He said, *SELF-MEDICATION IS THE WAY, NUMBING IS THE WAY*, and high-kicked his way to the medicine cabinet.

I think, *Go away*. I turn over, fluff my zillion pillows. He hounds me, he has an excess of crackling energy and apparently this is some sort of festival time I am unaware of, like holidays in Europe. After trying to sleep for an hour and failing, I open my eyes. I know what I have to do, what I've been putting off and not facing: the past made manifest; the wedding photos and the love letters and the truths and the half-truths and the epistolary and photographic evidence of our love and illusory history and greasy secrets, packed in boxes in the storeroom. It wasn't enough just to remove them from the house, as I did the week after he left. No, they are still well within the property line.

And the lies. They must be dealt with. I am sleeping on top of them every night and I can hear them breathing beneath the thin floorboards. Sometimes they hum country-western love songs, sometimes she-done-him-wrong songs, sometimes just accusatory silence. They know.

I think, *I finish this now, I destroy some of this now, I act now and I look at it all no matter what and I discard what was.* For me, this is heresy; this is severely against the feminine law of documentation and keepsakes and small priceless treasures. But I know what I know and those memory boxes are strangling me from the basement, little roots of hope springing through the rotting wood and soil, tentacles of pain trying to snake themselves around my ankles. There is work to be done.

I don't know what force propels me but I suspect it is a face-off with my demons, a bold offensive move on my part. It is me versus the Sawed-Off Madman in twelve rounds. Winner takes all. Irrational, determined, I get up; grab my yellow Eveready torchlight and head toward the storeroom like some grim maid of the night. Down to the storeroom I went. Down the back stairs in my frilly old-lady nightgown, with a box of garbage bags.

It was just as awful as I imagined, yes. I can see why I've put this off. It is excruciating to see those photographs, to see the old N, to see baby A in his arms at the hospital. To see apparent happiness on our faces at random cities, beaches, mountains, and houses. Everywhere. I couldn't screen the three large manila envelopes of our courtship e-mails; it would have taken too long. And once I started, could I have burned them? *Olly Olly Ice-Cream Free,* as A says.

There was so much, I stopped going through the separate photos and just threw them by the packet into the trash bags. So many little funny drawings N made when he used to be funny, bunches of small handwritten notes and cards where he said *Forever,* and *I adore you.* Seven years' worth, then—nothing. *Through thick and thin,* he wrote that too. So many of those little cards that go with flowers. There were a lot of flowers, it appears.

I had saved everything. I quite objectively judge myself a fool, an idiot, an imbecile, a sop, a dolt, a tacky bovine cow-figurine-woman who saved everything, while N sashayed off, without a single memory or photograph, glad to be rid of it all, glad to be rid of me. And sweet lil' organized me, with everything packed nicely in boxes, waiting for what? For the future, I had thought. For our old age, I'd thought.

Ashes, ashes, all fall down. The recent way A sang this in my presence . . . this may partially explain the mode of destruction, this sudden arson madness, the need to remove dangerous props and evidence from the cold files.

In the end I got it winnowed down to one box, one small box of memories, ruthlessly edited. I wanted to do better; at the end I was saying aloud, "It's too much. I'm sorry I can't do better. I just can't." I saved one or two very small things for the time capsule that leads to the wedding album. One or two or three bread crumbs for A to follow.

Up the stairs from the storeroom I go, dragging the two garbage bags, like an inverted Santa Claus in bare feet and my nightgown smeared with my tears and mucus. I begin to burn things. It's a truism that once you start burning, it takes on a life of its own, a frantic, fascinating momentum. After I burn a few items in the fireplace I think, *This venue is way too limited.*

Fire up the barbecue, I think. Yes. The Weber kettle. Outside. Everything is safer outside, especially things involving fire. A few minutes later, I fan out a heap of Match Light burning coals with a long stick, having formed a pyramid of ready-oiled coals first. From a foot above the coals to avoid the flames, I drop the iron grill atop the coals: a perfect shot.

"Now," I say out loud. I try not to speak, but I did say that one word. An incantation to the present and a curse to the past.

As the foundation, I use our marriage certificate, and then I lay all his love letters on top and anything in his handwriting, etc. Small flower notes were perfect as kindling. All untrue, all trash, all burned into ash. I want to rub the ashes into my skin, to swallow the past whole. Too many memories, and him out there with no memories at all. What a lucky brain N has, to not remember anything, to just be able to Empty Trash. Empty Family.

That is his right. I have mine. The right to burn, to raze the earth, and perhaps to start again. This is a call to action. I need the energy that is locked in these mementos. I need it all back.

I gently dismantle my carefully dried wedding bouquet, which has, I see now, bonus points, because the seamstress had sewn a piece of the chiffon veil as the bouquet tie, and also of course the satin ribbon itself. As I dropped them, they floated daintily in the blaze. A kind of ruination ballet, especially the long thin hemmed piece of silk chiffon. Crane vellum wedding invitations burn nicely also, the tissue divine.

There are *always* extra wedding invitations. A practical side of me is alert and taking notes: This solves the question of what to do with all those old extra wedding invitations. The Crane envclopes I carefully set aside for A to draw on. Or to use to write to his father in the insane asylum. Or to his mother at same. There is no question but that A will need these fine excellent envelopes.

The fire was high.

And I burned it all, including the one photo of the beautiful Thing Woman, which the Betty Lady found in between the drawers of N's desk. I watch her crumple and blacken. The neighbors are asleep and so didn't notice a large fire blazing in a huge Weber, and a woman in a Lansing nightgown bobbing and mincing about the flames. There was an amazing amount of fire and detritus, for so little a love.

I don't even recognize those people, I think, snatching glances at the photographs as they curl and smoke. They die too. Many of them never even called to ask how I was, or to acknowledge the event in any way; they simply acted as if I had died and A had died also. So. It's not all bad. A's birth announcements I kept. Those too. Last dance. For A, I kept the wedding album, and the one box. Inside that, my wedding band. For A's future wife, or no one.

In my mind, I go the other way with it, toward life far away: If there had been no A, I would have left the United States, moved to Paris. I would have outrun N and his new family. I could have. But he left me here to raise his son. A will always love N and vice versa, that much is certain. They are blood kin and alike in beautiful, striking ways. Their hairlines. Their thumbs. Their gift for jokes and drawing and making people feel at ease. Their zealous enthusiasm for small, cunning objects.

Somehow I needed to clean the ashes from the fireplace where it all began. I waited until they were cool.

I drifted off around five a.m. Eyes swollen shut. Limbs weak as though I'd tried to outrun a train and lost, though I did purge something. My hair smells of fire.

At least I am not hungover, I think upon waking; I like to look at the bright side. I also feel it was necessary, whatever has passed: Gallstone? Heart stone? It was necessary. Crazy but necessary, like so much of what works.

Unconsciously, I choose all white clothing the next morning and scatter the ashes onto the thickly woven trees behind the house, where nothing can grow. *I can tell you the past is a bucket of ashes*. Carl Sandburg.

If A ever asks me about divorce when he is grown up, especially if he has children, I will tell him what I know about this time when my spouse left and I was alone, the adult responsible for a baby.

I will say: "You enter into—well. You enter into a kind of madness. You will make discoveries, not all of them happy. And the surprises are not staggered or regularly spaced, they are coming at you at light-speed, all at once, and you have to continue. You don't get to stop and say, I'll pick this all up in a year or so, when it isn't so difficult or painful or scary. When I'm ready. No no no. You have to go back in daily, until. Until it passes, or something happens to lessen its dark brilliance. You never know when this will be. You just have to keep meeting it. And gradually it disperses, leaving a small tear in your heart. A little hole, an aperture in you, as in a camera lens which, in the right light, can be perceived and accepted as a perspective-enhancing hole. *A discontinuity allowing passage*: That's the definition of a hole. You find that it's something you can easily live with, that it affords the reciprocal nature of light and dark in even measure. You learn that it can be a life-enhancing gift, and not just a wound taken in a heart-game called marriage. Finally, you understand that the game isn't to get your husband back, or to get a new one. The game is to get free."

And Grief recedes into its dank alley, smoking a Gauloise.

V
Acceptance

The moment of change is the only poem.

—Adrienne Rich

Soup

I gained my ex husband, N, with soup. Not charm, wit, or lingerie, but soup. Not canned soup or deli, but real homemade soup, simmered for hours over a hot Jenn-Air. The kind of soup that makes your eyes roll back in your head and your body feel, for a brief time, safe.

I used to carry it to his first modest office in coy shopping bags with handles, laden with my own Tupperware bearing split pea with ham, or vegetarian black-eyed pea. Fresh soup delivered to his office in professional yet saucy outfits, while his coworkers teased and he strutted like a Rhode Island Red. Also consider the source: I was a paid professional myself, a writer; I bore soup made from scratch, which includes soaking the beans overnight. At the time, this seemed roughly akin to raising a barn.

I believe my deceptively simple cabbage and rice soup, finished off with handfuls of Gruyère cheese and oversize garlic croutons, is the one that sent him over the edge. He has admitted as much. The cabbage soup stands as the last crumbling brick in the wall of his bachelorhood. It explains how he was blinded into a formal commitment, despite his horror regarding legal matters. He was especially fearful of marriage, which he filed in his mental ledger of liability just below malpractice and above loan default.

N could overcome the lure of my smooth, naked legs draped casually over his, the good mutual taste of each other. The conversations. He could handle the ambrosia of a new lover and all the mindless meandering that entailed, but he could not physically get past the delicious, sedative comfort of my soup repertoire. By premeditated design, I was inexorably attached to the soup. I was the mistress of the soup. I was the god of the soup. I could giveth or taketh away.

In N's life, as disciplined as he attempted to make it, the soup had gone from a Want to a Need. He was hooked, an unfortunate yet apt phrase. A shiny male, a many-colored fish trying to live the free life another day. The ornate wrasse.

In the beginning I was on my best and most false behavior in many aspects, as was N. The making of the soup was just the tip of the iceberg. We sought the intersection of all senses, the folding together of sex and of wardrobe and the fey territory of bread pudding in whiskey sauce. We avoided all areas of conflict. Instead, elaborate rituals were made, based on erotic and dining preferences. It was the time of organic arugula and jicama and all manner of exotic vegetables and delicacies, served in the dim restaurants where candles wink on white tablecloths, and coarse sea salt sits in a cunning tiny bowl. We ate out often in the beginning, better to admire each other over a wee marble table. We perched, deuce after deuce, in small cafés, holding hands while the waiter discreetly avoided us, knowing his tip would be large, as all possibility is at the onset of love.

This is the time when metropolitan women such as myself will happily scrub their underutilized efficiency-apartment kitchens, rolling up sleeves on carefully toned and suntanned arms. An apron will be purchased, maybe two. The cornucopia of the lightest and freshest seasonal ingredients appears; butcher shops with the finest meats and fish will be ransacked. Potatoes, if they are ever seen, will be thinly sliced and crisply fried and seasoned with fresh sage; new potatoes may appear, just two or three nestled against moistly grilled king salmon.

I prepared all manners of dishes as though born to it. If pressed for time, I would remove gourmet food from takeout tins and fob it off as my own. I decided it would be best to lie; it really was just the smallest bit of chicanery, nothing like the real farce our marriage would contain. I didn't know this yet. I was still smashing tinfoil takeout cartons into the trash and covering them up with the outer leaves of romaine lettuce. This woman seems very disturbed, now. I am not afraid of my garbage anymore.

In the beginning, I was bending over backward and doing high-kicks to demonstrate how wonderful and well tempered and smart I was, yet in a nonthreatening way. N would slip silently from bed to fetch coffee and serve it up bedside, exactly as I like it. Our life was rife with soft Bach sonatas and flaky croissants and bud vases with a single stalk of freesia. Cloth napkins were whipped out for every single meal, not a paper towel in sight. There was much serving of coffee and tea and even breakfast in bed, along with the morning *Times* and an insouciant smile. We were both losing weight despite drinking wine like water and eating fat-laden foods. I put this down to the sex: Appetite fans out and succumbs to carnal recreation.

N began, methodically and with many flourishes, to plan intimate at-home dinners for two, making sure that I understood that this was something he only did when he was truly in love. He chose the music with care. I am afraid I gasped, realizing he loved the same obscure vocalist I happened to also love. N's pans, however, remained in his kitchen, the Cuisinart tucked in its usual corner of the immaculate marble counter.

N could debone a chicken, perfectly whole, in five minutes, leaving the chicken itself intact but spineless. Instead of alarming me, this thrilled me. I thought it was a magical impossibility. It's amazing what clues I missed, and what I treasured. Equally amazing is how easily it can be let go, in the fullness of time. But this was the beginning, the inky genesis. What Edna St. Vincent Millay would call " the dry seed of most unwelcome this."

If not for the middle, I would never have known the contentment of serving *my husband*, N, the last lamb chop while he speaks of my accomplishments in glowing terms. Mornings he makes coffee, although gone are the days of nice sticky pastries, and the bud vase has somehow gone missing. It matters not, we are in the middle and life is rattling right along, together with the plain stoneware dishes in the dishwasher (the better dishes and thin-stemmed crystal goblets are once again relegated to special occasions). Our bodies trade fine restaurants for bustling diners and coffeehouses. His good pans now commingle with mine, the Cuisinart in my possession. I'd gained Cuisinart. This was everything. I felt my work done and that I should be afforded rest. This does not happen; nothing ever rests right in the middle. It is almost impossible to balance a scale for this very reason.

We have begun to eat off each other's plates, this in itself tantamount to commitment of a primal nature. The middle means marriage, and sharing, it also means opening up to the grinchy day-to-day reality and all it contains. We talk about The Marriage now, as if it were a fairly nice person in another room. Everything is buzzing along like bees making honey, and yes, like bees, everything seems to be, well, kind of a lot of work. Yes, we have started using paper napkins, but only because we are married now and it is just too much trouble to send the laundry out that often. Of course it is.

In fact, the stomach is still connected to the heart during the middle, but not in as direct a fashion. Now all impulses must pass through the brain, and so we are a wee bit more cautious with both our napkins and our heavy cream, a little afraid to gain weight now that the sex is down to once every two days—still a startling amount! And who can deny the comfort of being able to eat dinner in front of the television? No one. Once baby A arrives and eventually outgrows the "football in a bucket" phase, this is reinforced and one or the other of us begins trying to get away. *Oh no, let ME be the one to run to the store for butter. No, I insist. But you got to go to the store last time. I need to get some air.* Everyone needs additional air.

The middle is a different kind of feast, the slow and easy kind, the casual kind that doesn't require stiletto heels or crisp shirts. There are some disturbances in the field (he hates my art collection, I hate his art collection), but nothing that cannot be solved with a fat bottle of Merlot, a bucket of steamers, thigh-high stockings, a low-cut blouse, and a little coaxing.

The middle is nice. It is a pity it cannot last longer. I have heard tales of couples staying in the middle for decades, of favorite dishes being served every Sunday, family lobster feasts, and dependable anniversary dinners at A. Sabella's. It hasn't been so for me, nor for many of my contemporaries, some of who have run the entire food-and-love gamut several times without bearing children or even jewelry of any true worth. Sadly, now I know with a bittersweet thump that I will try love again; appetite is a constant. The more I say I won't, the closer my desire creeps behind me.

The end, when it comes, will be heralded by the cessation of all romantic dinners whisked to small tables by officious waiters. Gone are the days of the constructed salads and butterflied lamb rack, and as for the homemade soup? It is extinct. One may try making soup at the End, but it will not have the same effect, and in fact if the stamina exists at all, it is probably mania or terror in disguise. Soup will be scorned. More likely one or both of us is hunched over a bowl of Thai noodles, while the other is on the computer in another room, with the door closed. *The door closed.* Does this ring any bells? I don't refer to wedding bells. Hemingway bells.

If meals are shared, it is with the television on and loud. This to avoid discussions of The Marriage, which neither wants to broach any longer, as it has become a rather unreliable and dangerous character. Meals have slipped into the realm of the ordinary and the grim—frozen shrimp, overcooked chicken parts, including dark meat (there is no dark meat in the Beginning, only breasts). Iceberg lettuce appears like a weather-beaten old friend, along with bottled salad dressing, slapped down on the coffee table along with an array of other condiments that really cannot perform the kind of magic that would transform these silent meals into anything but ghastly and penitentiary-like. I would silently reminisce about the time of holding hands over a plate of warm goat cheese with chutney and watercress and candied walnuts, but there is no chutney. The sparkling conversationalist, N, has turned into a monosyllabic drone; the male gourmand is now unable to find a stick of butter in plain sight and complains openly about the ratio of vodka to vermouth in his martini, which I continue to make for him, like the butler in a Jack Benny comedy hour. I've become Rochester.

True, I had let myself go in the area of the nurturing domestic, as evidenced by the fact that standing very near to the dishwasher while the Dry Cycle steam rises from its vent is as close as I've come to home-cooking in a long time. I no longer buy his favorite cheese at the market; in fact, I wouldn't know it if I saw it, because my eyes have gone slitty from trying to tell if he is lying about those long lunches. He in turn will watch me for signs of sexual abandon but will find none there; the day the coffee in bed went, so did my insatiable urge for fellatio. Yes, we had reached the end. No more track, baby. End of the line; feel free to take this train back to your point of origin, if you can, which you definitely cannot.

Since the divorce, I acknowledge that I don't control which way the metaphysical bread is going to fall, butter side up or down. With this kind of mystery and the overall shortness of life, serious long-held regrets have no place. It is better to just wait and see. Hang on tight to that bread. Accept. Not for anyone else, naturally. For A and me, for what I recognize with a certain satisfaction is our family.

Here in Marin County, acceptance is socially mandated, so that I and hundreds of other ex wives can continue, without undue delay, to consume material goods. We dutifully resume raising the children, alone and with competence. We pay everyone and their cousin exorbitant amounts of money to maintain our preposterously small houses; we write in our journals, and eventually, after a socially mandated time, live to sauté mushrooms again. Once again survival, evolution, and most of all transience reigns, as Darwinian and predestined as it ultimately is. Change is assessed and refinanced, as are our homes.

After I married N and became a mother, the Mallomars arrived in the kitchen, after a goodly twenty-year absence. And there was much inner dancing and rejoicing and dipping into coffee and stuffing into my mouth. But one day the Mallomars had no power. I had gained seniority. I am still tired of the Mallomars. Truth be told, I could live very happily without ever seeing a Mallomar again.

I don't dwell on getting back together with N. He's become my Mallomar. This is acceptance, and it's very normal and natural and entirely impossible until you've had that very last fat black cookie.

The Marriage Plays

N brought up four loads of firewood from the basement to burn through the cool, wet spring, and fixed a few things around the house. He is now happy to do what he can to improve this environment, to earn his presence. I never have to ask twice or await follow-through.

Divorce has its upside, I see. Men will change their behavior in order to be included in the swing of things.

N says, smiling, "So basically you just want me to take down your sheers from the curtain rods, put up your rain-forest showerhead, and not of course pretend to be your lover or intimate friend."

"That's pretty much it," I say, wiping my forehead with a red bandanna. "The sheers are filthy."

N: "Uh-huh."

"It's just something I need two people for. No one tall has come over lately . . . plus, they're dusty and dirty. It's not something you'd really ask a friend to do."

"But since I'm not a friend, I can do it."

"Exactly. Yes. Also there is the toilet seat project; as you know, N, it's custom and I can't find a match at the Ace hardware store. All the same reasons apply, I can't ask anyone else to do it. That toilet seat is a goner. I just can't take it another day. And I know you can do it," I explain.

"Well, of course you can't find it at Ace. That's because you have to take it off its hinge and go to the designer outlet in San Anselmo, by that French laundry. . . ."

I do miss N's capabilities when he is unavailable. But it's his very capabilities that have slain the marriage. As in, capable of anything.

I inhale N's scent; we are at ease with each other, as we were in our first blush of living together. And we are unmarried. We have had an ugly divorce, and I can still become angry with him. And yet. Is there something in the wedding ceremony that actually is binding in some ethereal and nonspecific fashion? Something ineffable that stays just at the edge of the divide? What is this emotional marbling of familiarity and affection and support that flows between us, even now, beyond the legal obliteration?

I muse how it is very difficult to completely, emotionally and psychically, un-marry—even with divorce—especially if there's a child. The couple has a blood bond, no matter the status of connubial intimacy.

It may be that a marriage, with an infant, a marriage that has been interrupted and ultimately bested by an affair, needs and will take the time—no matter what and despite best or worst intentions—to have its natural ending.

Is that why I tried to get N back, and why he put up with it despite his obvious preference for another? Yes. The marriage had to come to its natural conclusion. And that had a date, in the same way a wedding has a date, and not the date that any of us decided. The institution had to taper off over a period of time not revealed in the legal documents: an impossible, invisible clause, a parcel of time that can't be court-ordered, planned, known, or skipped.

The marriage plays itself out, despite human determination.

Absolutely Impersonal

Lisa and I are walking through the food court in Macy's, which somehow has been taken over by a few kiosks owned by Wolfgang Puck or someone just like him. It's just terrifying. I remember when they had a restaurant. Change, oh yes, I understand now. It's further change, and it's absolutely impersonal.

Lisa asks me if I'm hungry, if I ate breakfast. I tell her that I had a rib eye for dinner last night, which, like a cobra, I'm still digesting. I can feel it, moving in a noticeable mass through my large intestine.

Lisa says, "You're eating steak? You're completely over him."

I can speak freely with Lisa. Lisa is safe harbor, she is also in her forties and thus has considered everything.

I ask her, "So what is N now? I don't like the sound of *ex*. It sounds like a variable. Does he revert back to friend?"

"I don't think so," Lisa says, deep in thought.

"Father of my child?"

"I suppose. Yes, that's the cleanest."

"N says I am still a person he can *really* talk to," I tell her.

"Bullshit," Lisa says.

We look at each other and open our eyes wide.

"I KNOW," I say, grinning.

"PLEASE," Lisa says, holding both of her hands up, fingers splayed.

That night I make quick Indian food for A and Lisa, using the tikka masala canned sauce, with stupendous results. Single mothers, I reflect, are free from the tyranny of large pale birds and unmanageable slabs of red meat and the enslavement of the kitchen. This dish took sixty minutes, only because the brown rice was obstinate. Is brown rice something I am going to deal with in the future? No, it is not.

We are all three wearing hooded sweatshirts, it is tribal. We are about to get into the car to drive to my parents' house when A stops. Tilts his head back and strikes a pose.

"I'm smelling rain," he says.

"Does it smell good?" I ask.

"Yes."

I tilt my neck upward. He's right.

"Oh," Lisa says, throwing her head back. "Wicked."

We all examine the sky. We decide it is frightening to the west, and there may yet be a rainbow. The idea is enough.

We drop A at Bunny's, and drive back over the Bay Bridge into San Francisco for a night out.

Lisa and I catch up on adult talk over Irish coffees. A trio is setting up on the tiny stage at Café du Nord. I feel a sense of expansion; I never thought I'd see this room again. It used to be blocks from my last single-girl apartment; I brought every date here. The club looks as macabre and threadbare as before; a great place to meet Lisa for a session. Here there is no fee, no fifty-minute perimeter . . . also goodness and mercy are considered irrelevant.

I express to Lisa how I appreciate her and her husband's boycotting N and his association to Thing Woman.

Lisa gives me the Dial Tone Look, to express her general outrage.

Ehhhhhhhhhhhhhhhhhhhhhhhh.

She says, "Don't mention it. Let me tell you something good about tonight, Chickweed."

I smile and relax in my tatty chair.

"You're not waiting for some betrayer to come home talking trash to you. You're not sitting there trying to look pert and sexy and happy as a spiffed-up vegetable so that he won't call the mistress—or at least one hopes. Fruitlessly. You are being your authentic self, or at least a reasonable facsimile, and you aren't on the bad end of the truth stick while N creeps off to some lair for a tryst. No. You don't PLAY that.

"That's what's good about tonight," Lisa concludes.

"Damn," I say. A little bark of a laugh escapes me. I feel refreshed, as if my oxygen tanks have just been changed. I could run around the block ten times.

"The truth," Lisa says, "waits for eyes unclouded by longing."

I wait.

"Unknown Chinese philosopher," Lisa says, undulating her fingers in the air above her head.

"Should I go to Paris?" I suddenly ask Lisa. It's been on my mind, a lurking need to continentally reset.

"Do you have the money?"

"No."

Lisa nods, as if this is a prerequisite.

"But I have the miles, just simmering in my United Mileage Plus account. Eighty thousand."

Lisa nods again. Having any less would be tragic in Lisa's world, like being homeless.

"Is this an evolved act, or is it selfish escapism?" I ponder this and wave in another round of Irish with a wide swing of my arm. "Also—I have to think about A . . ."

Lisa raises her eyebrows high.

"Is it morally right to do such a thing and leave A for six days, in order to follow my own bliss? God, I hate that expression."

"It is perfectly hateful," Lisa agrees.

"In short . . . ," I ask, sucking the foam off my drink, ". . . what would Jesus do?"

"Well," Lisa says. "I don't think Jesus had the miles to go to Paris."

Deny Everything

"I'll deny it, but sometimes I'm scared about this new baby . . . ," N says a few days before I leave for Paris. He says this as he is twisting his head around to change the filter on my furnace. I am watching so I will know how to do it the next time.

I think these words would have meant something before. Their stock has plummeted.

"No matter what happens, don't hate me." He opens his arms to hug me. Ah. He's going for the fraternal body press. A good move.

I go Blank. I allow the embrace. It is primitive, the need to hug, I muse. Yet I know it is momentary, based on blood mingled in A and our ropy connection through time. Is that love? No. And N has a new baby coming now.

I step away.

Later, I'm in the bathtub talking to N, who is calling on the thinnest of pretense about A. He subtly accuses me of shanghai-ing the new pajamas he bought for A to stay at his place. He has lost the pajamas and he is freaking out, so he also subtly accuses me of turning A against him, which is patently absurd because A adores his father; if anything, I talk N up to his son.

"Look, I didn't steal any pajamas. Don't be mad at me. I am completely benign and passive," I say, beginning to laugh. "I just sat here while you divorced my ass."

"I know. I know. You shouldn't have let me divorce you," N jokes. I hear a hair dryer in the distance. Thing Woman.

Unfortunately, what N says is not true, and we both know it. I did everything I could to stop the divorce, to not let it happen. Which was wrong, like trying to stop a tornado. I should have said, *Get thee behind me, Satan*. Instead, I said, *Get thee in front of me, Satan. After you, Lucifer.*

As for me poisoning A against N? Maybe A just has not yet properly shown that he has noticed N's leaving or keened enough, though Lord knows I have done my share. Still. In N's deepest wish, A is running swiftly to the door, as he used to. A doesn't run for his father as much, probably a function of age. But he's very glad to see him, at a walk.

"I have to go, I have something in the oven," I say, and hang up. Never mind that there are library books in the oven.

I don't have to win back or replace N to get his benefits (few but novel). It seems he will be hanging about, anyway, in spirit and phone and e-mail, like a mad landlord. He sits on my porch when he drops A off, like he still lives here, but he doesn't have a key. He's not an indoor dog anymore. Whole days go by without my really thinking of him. He's out there somewhere, but not in my immediate aegis. I am beginning to notice other men, I begin to see that love is not in competition with faithlessness or treachery at all, that they are separate entities altogether. I can choose only one and not the other, at any time.

Soon enough, I open my hands and weigh love . . . or treachery. Love or treachery. After a few heart-piercing lessons, I understand that treachery is not at love's left hand. I am lucky to learn this at forty-one, I know it. I've regained control of myself; I exist. It's enough if I say it is.

I exist single or coupled, at any age, in any age. N didn't give it to me, and he can't take it away.

Bling

My passive-aggressive ex-coworker/friend Brianna (who has in reality joined N's new camp and is no longer my friend) surprises me for coffee downtown. I've walked to the Depot Café Bookstore in Mill Valley, ordered coffee, and sat down to review my column notes; and there she is, hovering. Much like a brown house spider, Brianna has been loitering at the periodical rack and waiting patiently. She offers to sit down with me and talk. I become a zombie and nod. Part of me wants to know everything about Thing Woman and the pregnancy, right down to her brand of toothpaste and the fetus's movement, and the other part is sucking a shotgun and gesturing madly to the ammunitions officer.

Brianna sits down with me and explains about serial monogamy and how the single marriage is dead, how serial monogamy is the way. I consider telling her that N and I had sex together, but she is not leaving an opening, is serving hard and fast.

She continues to speak; she feels that despite my pain, I should acknowledge the courage of N's decision to walk away from his unhappiness and free A and me from being unhappy as well.

"I'm not sure I'd call it courage," I say. "Firemen are courageous. Police are courageous."

Then I see it. She flashes me her new engagement ring, four carats if it's a gram. She announces her engagement to Mateo, a nice teacher man whom I now will certainly never see again.

"That's a beautiful ring," I say truthfully.

"Thank you. Mateo gave it to me on Christmas Eve. And I'm sure N will be marrying his girlfriend, too. But I'm getting married first."

I congratulate her with a small hug. If I had an X-Acto knife I might plunge it into her back or my own; this is why I don't carry X-Acto knives, though they are handy and precise.

She looks at her ring, sighs happily, and then gets back on jury duty.

"Well, I understand why you'd feel that way about N not being courageous. I'll honestly have to think more about that. For now—well, I know it's a cliché, but Valentine's Day could be the big day. But no one really knows . . . ," she says, ruminating. "Maybe they don't want to wait."

"No, I wouldn't wait if I were them," I say, mouth frozen, pursed.

In this way, I receive the rumor that N will marry Thing Woman. This while my own son has to call his father on the telephone to see if he still likes the smell of gasoline. In the buzzing sound that is all around me, all this news goes in one ear and out the other, like a long knitting needle. I've lost fully and sincerely. It's not so bad. *Just keep moving,* my mind says.

"It's best for all concerned," says Brianna. "That's the highest good any of us can ask for."

I say nothing. I am stunned enough to ignore the baskets of crusty bread rolls and the curls of sweet butter, which she ignores because she is also going to be married soon. I see the artful rolls and the beautiful butter, dotted with moisture. I see Brianna's ring. It sparkles. It announces itself.

She actually tries to take my hand with her left hand: the one with the bling. I know she would like me to touch the ring. Kiss the ring.

I stand and reach for my wallet. Feets don't fail me now.

"Congratulations," I say. "Surely the best years are still to come."

I pause to lay down a ten for the coffee, tax, and gratuity. There is no need to calculate the small change.

I stride by the other diners, gaining speed. I gently push the door marked Exit.

The Highly Symbolic Transcontinental
Sojourn of the Recently Divorced

After eighteen months and one divorce, something is bent within me that must be straightened. In Paris.

At the U.S. airport I think, What am I out to prove, achieve? Phantom pain pangs and the free-falling anxiety woo woo. I think to myself, *This is crazy, me going there. I am a single mother now.* Yet there seems a debt I must pay myself.

Paris has no place for fear; it doesn't exist unless imported. I have not brought any fear. The near worst that could happen has happened, and this frees me.

This favorite hotel is the best in my price range, and ideally located in the Latin Quarter. Facts are still facts, as I recently rediscovered, like lost earrings. Nothing in the settlement provides against Paris, most especially nothing in my heart prevents it from singing as I see the Panthéon. This is my fourth trip; I will continue to visit Paris throughout my life, by hook or by crook. I will steal, if necessary. I will rob and pillage and embezzle. I think it will come to that, and I'm prepared to do whatever necessary to keep this city in my life. N preferred Italy, particularly Sienna, a town surrounded by walls. Big, thick, impenetrable walls with a long history of knights and soldiers and peasants gathered within, generally torturing, gaming, and beating the life out of one another.

I am in France, I think. I can wear a sarong and a silk T-shirt to dinner, alone. I can go over the top with shoes. Go ahead and order the *poulet grille* and not something more elaborate, as N would have insisted upon; he was particularly susceptible to capers and truffles. No capers, and I can use large amounts of butter, which is impossible to find just yards away in Italy. I cannot request ketchup for the *pomme de terre,* the french fries, facts being facts.

This trip, I know the way to the Restaurant Polidor, down the raised street with three steps at its curb, and the fact that the guidebooks are wrong. I have to keep going straight up rue de prince, I never turn. I know that I'll find the Polidor just as I'm giving up hope.

Le Polidor, three stars in the *Gault Millau Guide.* Long, family-style tables with red-checked oilcloth, carafes of water. The house wine, the *vin du modis,* is written in curly script on glass walls that surround the room. *Le pichet* 8E, *le pot* 11E, Domaine du Tracot, a delicious red. I note that the hostess has grown more beautiful, with ankle-laced sandals and a large silver six-pointed star on a necklace at her white throat. Zaftig, she glides. Her face is the face of this restaurant. A close second are the stern faces of the flinty, spry twin sisters in their seventies who wait tables, their identical wire-framed glasses glinting like those of the gods, the white aprons specially twisted at the back and tied with a knot. White aprons over white Le Polidor T-shirts. Always.

The patroness seats me at the far end of the long table, next to the bread-chopping station. Chop chop chop. It is too appropriate; therefore I must get up and change seats, to the other edge of the table across the way. There is a tall wicker bread hamper holding long baguettes in brown paper bags; they feel like tall, nameless acquaintances, warm and friendly and at my service. Similar loaves line the long spiral staircase that leads to the cellar.

The single men do not sit on the edges, I notice. They are placed in the middle, like centerpieces.

A cell phone rings. No cell phone for me here, another measure of safety. I am floating, a pod, an observing capsule in space. A man with a pipe speaks animatedly to his blond wife, who I notice much later is a dwarf. Paris is marvelous. Next to this couple are two German women who have also been consigned to the edge. Here people talk to laugh; this is so unlike American large cities, where people talk to be seen talking. Also at the Polidor there is an apparently bottomless back room, where soccer players and families of fix or six are ushered. *BONJOUR, MADAM,* they shout out, known.

I can smoke between courses. What a delightful country, I think again. I order another small pichet of the excellent house wine. I settle in, obstinate. The cassis-soaked cake is not to be missed under any circumstances. Their specialty.

The plump patroness with long blond hair—thick, substantial hair and bangs—packed in a tight black cotton dress, suddenly smiles at me: I have shown initiative by changing seats while she was otherwise engaged. Also by staying for dessert. Why do I feel I am home? I wonder but am not engaged in a solution to this question.

After dinner, I roll gratefully downhill to the Panthéon and also my hotel. I sleep for sixteen hours. Breakfast is brought to my room: croissant, café au lait. A single soft-boiled egg, which I ordered fried; luckily they botched the order, or else they just disagreed with it. Here, I must give in to the fact that ultimately the French know better. I drink that peculiar tart orange juice that is a grapefruit-orange-hybrid brew, magic; it completely erases all effects of prior wine.

To this issue of drinking at every single lunch and dinner, the French government has a poster on the outside hotel wall:

> **Attention! L'alcool tue lentement.**
> **Beware! Alcohol kills slowly.**

Someone has scrawled graffito thereon:

> **On s'en fout. On n'est pas pressé.**
> **We don't care. We're not in a hurry.**

The Vagabond

The next morning I leave the hotel at ten a.m. in a white T-shirt and spandex shorts, backless sky blue Nikes. I might as well be wearing a kilt, I appear so foreign. The petite French women in their raw silk green blazers are having none of it. They raise their eyes most insultingly, but I care not. The men look longingly at my exposed legs; they are suntanned and have long muscles, as I am sure did Sisyphus. I'm so bare and it is September, after the end of summer, which the French declare August 31, and rightfully so, according to fashion. I am witch, harlot. All just by wearing exercise shorts.

I plan to reread *The Vagabond* today during café stops; will gleefully immerse myself in Colette, not for the first time. Like an old lover, Colette is waiting for me in my hotel room.

When I first started out on my all-day walk around Paris, my immediate thought was: I was younger then; I cannot do this any more. Too much trekking. My heart is racing and my calves ache. This after one block.

Five hours later I return to the hotel, blistered but unbowed. I walk ten miles a day here, maybe fifteen. I am alive here, I think. But what am I, neither wife nor mother? Madam. I am Madam. Good-bye, Mademoiselle.

At the hotel, they are remodeling. No accidents. I was given a small room overlooking the Panthéon, as requested in my faxed reservation. A small room, yet charming. The French pull off a small room in a way that others can't. The high windows that open. Good heavy drapes with sheers, window boxes with real flowers. The nineteenth-century art prints. The bidet, a deep tub. Oh, and the Panthéon. They compensate, the French. The crooked van Gogh bed, worn but tough. The good sheets. The armoire that locks.

During lunch at the nearby Brasserie Balzar, there is a table of four from the Bronx, seated next to me. Splendid people.

"We're touring this place," they say.

Across the room, Leslie Caron is seated. "That's Leslie Caron," they say.

"Yes," I say. "We're having a peak experience."

Next day, I do the Louvre, walking there after lunch. The statue of *Victoire de Samothrace* transfixes me: *Winged Victory*. No head, a woman with wings, shoulders held back and high, and what looks like a sarong flowing all about her. This says it all; she is my talisman.

At the Picasso museum I ask myself: If I were one of Picasso's women, which one would I be? Marie-Thérèse? No. Dora Maar. Probably. Jacqueline? At least she has claws, and a matching power presumably. In Picasso's self-portraits, I note that he gives himself a composure and confidence that his women rarely receive. My favorite painting is the *Weeping Woman,* the purple slash of color, her jagged, broken features: the perfect expression of kinetic despair. I'm glad this is no longer I, but it seems we nod infinitesimally at each other in silent recognition.

Small events begin to intercede on my seclusion; there are e-mails on my laptop and phone messages at the concierge desk. The world is starting to filter through the continental drift, the tentacles are reaching out.

It escalates, this tentacle effect. My magazine editor has taken the liberty of calling me in Paris requesting, on my guestroom voice mail, a few hundred words for my next project. . . . "Can you quickly, quickly jot down your keys to a Successful Divorce . . . you know . . . very Your Take on All of It, Suzanne, and don't be afraid to Surprise People."

I have bills to pay. I will say yes to this as I say yes to everything I am asked to do for money.

Editor wants these simple tips to be eventually printed on small oblongs of glossy paper for readers, like a tipping guide to carry in pocket or purse. These steady dribbles of work continue to drive me toward a practical, upbeat tempo. I focus on meeting the challenge of modern dissolution and avoiding financial ruin, social ostracizing, complete mental breakdown, homicide, assault charges, and tax crimes of an obtuse nature. "Going publicly insane," I suggest in one piece, "is not an option. There are standards of behavior to be met, several light-years below Edwardian standards, low standards but standards nonetheless. Look smart," I suggest. "Stagger your episodes and keep the wreaking of vengeance regularly spaced as well as surprising. A constant adversary is none at all. Step lively!" I take out a pen and begin to edit the requested master list over excellent coffee:

Ten Simple Yet Elegant Tips for Divorce

1. Change the locks.
2. Make him pay for the divorce—and anything else you can.
3. Keep everything beginning with consonants.
4. Allow him to keep everything beginning with vowels.
5. Sequester precious items at a friend's house. Men never remember what they have—if they did, they would not have ruined their lives by running around with whores.
6. Don't fight in front of the children. . . .

7. (. . . This includes your ex husband—it only adds gasoline to the fire, and they don't care how angry you are, truly they do not. This is because they exist wholly in their own tiny birdcage of a brain/genital control tower.)

8. Take lots of baths and get manicures and pedicures; have your hair expensively cut.

9. Everything, no matter how ludicrous and squalid it seems at the time of the split, will get better and better until you will wonder why you cared so much in the first place.

10. When confronted with a practical question regarding fairness to your ex, err on the side of lifetime vendetta. This way, you will never feel a fool and you will also have kept everything.

The Most Terrifying Place on Earth

I am at the Charles de Gaulle Airport in France, with an hour to kill. Duty-free takes on a magisterial glow, those two little words march forth and conquer wallets throughout the universe. I buy:

Yves Saint Laurent lipstick (3)
Multi-finish lipstick *(rouge personnel)* #18, forbidden plum *(prune interdit)*

Multi-finish lipstick (*rouge personnel*) #19, stylish brown
  (*brun chic*)
And pure transparent lipstick (*rouge pur transparent*) #7,
  SPF 8, sweet tea (*thé sucre*)
Estée Lauder pure color gloss trio (travel exclusive) 1 quartz,
  2 rhubarb, 5 copper
Selection of small and cunning Yves Saint Laurent perfumes
  in a golden box
Selection of mini nail lacquers by Estée Lauder
Opium parfum (large spray bottle)
En Joy, their latest fragrance. (Joy is Bunny's favorite, so I buy
  her a bottle of En Joy to surprise her. Bunny is difficult to
  surprise.)
Samsonite luggage cart
Musée d'Orsay art cards (2 boxes): Miró and Matisse
Kitchen magnet with half-finished Eiffel Tower photograph

As a lark, I check my messages back in the United States.
While I am listening, I gasp and drop the pay phone receiver as
if it has caught fire.

Something impossible has happened. A coworker has died.
Impossible.

I stand there a long time, trying to absorb this latest folly of
the gods.

Dead. Passed. Erased. Wiped off face of Earth.

Dark Victory

When I come back from Paris, both Christian and the Betty Lady are dressed in mourning, to support me and also as a reason to flee their jobs in L.A. and hang at the beach. The Betty Lady is dolled up. Black pillbox hat with veil, dark pumps, everything impeccable, very Dark Victory. He's put together a total look. Christian is insisting on coming. I know he's concepting for a made-for-TV movie about a family with severe early mortality rates; it's like location scouting for Christian. Also the Betty Lady needs an escort, so that means Christian. Betty Lady's been trawling through the Castro District shopping for XL elbow-length black gloves.

After I unpack and everyone is asleep, I mosey into my storeroom and open my wedding album. I feel no gouging sorrow, just a tilting nostalgia and affection for that girl who had no idea what marriage was, none. I see the joy in N's face and the softness as he looked at me under my veil. I see it all and it's right. I pocket a black-and-white picture, in a minuscule silver frame, of us dancing at our wedding; I bring it into the house. I put it in A's room. It may inform his heart.

Now that I've been to Paris, it becomes clear that I don't truly want N. This decision is reinforced when I realize he is now free, unmarried, and the thought fills me with uneasiness versus pleasure. Toothy crocodiles shambling down alleys, I think. Hungry crocodiles with the ability to weep.

Thing Woman has set me free, like the truth. I deserve happiness. And N will always be a part of my life, because of A: Nothing is perfect and nothing is wrong.

Blob

I come up from organizing the basement store room and discover my ex husband on the premises. He has dropped off our son markedly early, as usual, and is asleep on the comfy chair in the living room. A is watching *The Grim Adventures of Billy & Mandy*.

I flop down on the couch, exhausted and not caring that I have on no makeup or lipstick. It should be enough just to show, it is enough.

I whistle once.

N wakes up and groggily explains, "I always like to spend a few relaxing minutes here...."

"Yes," I say, whipping my glasses off. This way he is just a Blob. Except for a sliver, my own eyes are slanted closed, like a dragon's. "Spend a few minutes in what used to be your life. I can dig that," I add dryly.

"See you on the twenty-second," I announce, leaving a large

space for him to gather and remove himself. Everything appears to sigh heavily as he drives away. The house settles back into itself.

Afterward I pick up a small green book, some ancient Greek literature that I hope will explain life, in particular the active and perplexing war between the sexes. I will use whatever wisdom I find. I have many, many books.

Kierkegaard, for example, muses in "Love and Marriage," "We read in fairy tales about human beings whom mermaids and mermen enticed into their power by means of demoniac music. In order to break the enchantment it was necessary in the fairy tale for the person who was under the spell to play the same piece of music backwards without making a single mistake. This is very profound, but very difficult to perform, and yet so it is: The errors one has taken into oneself one must eradicate in this way, and every time one makes a mistake one must begin all over."

Or you can just haul their ass out the door, I say to the ceiling. This is a vast improvement on the introductory wanting to die phase. I've not wished for hospitalization for months now. All astonishing to me, as astonishing as the sound of my own laughter bouncing off the walls of the house I didn't have to sell after all.

I walk down the street in town and realize I can smell the leaves again. Moreover, I know I'm happy now in some kind of lurching way, far more at peace than the feeling of Compromise and Long Suffering, which leads nowhere. Yes, a simple contentment, not exactly happiness, but a lack of suffering. Not true happiness yet, but close enough . . . with happiness in clear view as a choice. The sensation is new and it grows.

With A now becoming a little person in full beingness, the panic is gone, the sheer cliffhanging emotion of divorce. There is a new settled feeling to my life with A. There is satisfaction in simply making life work; a roundness to everyday living that I was looking for all along, and found at the end of this debacle. N has somehow missed our boat . . . but it's all right for A and me. It is enough. I've come to a place of willing understanding that though we still can connect on demand, N has a new family, and there is no going back for either of us. Even if we both wanted to, the road back is no longer passable. The way is lost to us now.

N may have a deficient moral sensibility, but most people do. I had invested him with the power to make me happy, that's the kink of it. And the investiture can't be easily rescinded. And some of what I know is banal: e.g., there is only one cure for one man—and that's another man. I decide to pass, for now, and the die-alone anxiety is replaced by a kind of wry sense of inevitability and intrigue for what's born next. For truly I am leaving one life and beginning another, trying to take all the good, only that. Becoming whole again, even if some parts are maimed. Still, wholeness is somewhere I now know the way to, despite feckless shortcuts, disastrous detours, slight skirmishes, and the occasional trip wire of an almost malicious sweet memory.

I think, *He was this great armoire that I thought needed a little Liquid Gold, and turns out had a split up its back the width of a pencil.*

A beats the buttons out of me at cards, but not Bunny. A and Bunny have a face-off; Bunny wins.

"Pair of deuces. Ace high," Bunny announces, and slaps down her hand.

On the subject of future relationships, my mother has this to say: "I think you have a right to be bitter. I acknowledge bitterness. But you can't be bitter and move on, have another relationship."

"Why not?" I ask idly.

Bunny explains, "It would be bitter."

"Oh."

"It would be like trying to run two hoses through one connector. Impossible. You have to turn one off to get to the other. They can't exist in the same place."

I nod, pursing my lips into a moue.

Bunny: "Remember the parachuter's motto . . ."

"What's that?"

"Don't wait too long," my mother says.

Fall Down Twice

Last night I was in San Francisco at Christian's fortieth birthday party.

I dolled myself up and cruised into the Clift Hotel (designed by Ian Schrager, who would have had a place in the Gestapo, so severe and perfect are his lines). The Betty Lady had nicked a penthouse from the front desk; the Gay Mafia was involved. He paid something like $100 for the whole night, and it was nine hundred square feet. Everyone I love was there, except my son and my parents; in this case, a perfect omission.

The party mainly overtook the penthouse suite, strewn with black rose petals, which I have to assume were harvested from the gardens of Hades itself. There was a pitcher of mojitos and a crazy bald man who kept running around refilling drinks while no one was looking, so everyone thought they had one drink and really they had ten or twelve.

Toward the end of the evening, I sat in the 3X-scale Louis XIV chair in the lobby of the Clift Hotel, like a sassy doll on a high chair. I shouted across the lobby to Lisa and the Betty Lady and Christian and his new girlfriend, and they took pictures of me and shouted back. We cleared the lobby within minutes and took right over, spreading into the Redwood Room Bar toward the end of things.

Mothers do not clear lobbies unless their child has gone missing and they are hysterical. I was hysterical, but not with fear: with joy.

The party was so good, I fell down on the floor laughing. Twice. Once on the balcony, laughing at a joke that a drag queen named FiFi had just made involving a false-bottom vase and a succulent plant. And once in the elevator, going down on the way out, riding down with two semi-famous designers.

We had mistakenly ridden the service elevator down after leaving the grand penthouse, and when the doors opened we looked out into some horrible industrial yellow place, deep in the bowels of the hotel, where a dwarf with a stiff white chef's hat yelled at us in Spanish.

And in that moment, the whole carefully constructed aesthetic of the evening was ruined, which struck us all as unbearably funny and when we went up one floor to the lobby in the right elevator, we spilled out into the lobby, just fell out of the elevator as though our legs had been cut out from underneath us. We were instant quadriplegics, it seems.

We decided to share a room and spend the night at the Clift, after the last fall. In the end, we realized that driving two-thousand-pound vessels of steel after a tsunami of tequila wasn't the best of plans. My neighbor girl, Hannah, agreed to spend the night, for an extra fifty dollars, the deal of the century.

In the morning and upon my arrival back home, A runs happily to me and says that a leprechaun jumped into the bathroom window last night.

"Do you believe in leprechauns?" he asks me.

"Oh yes, certainly. I believe in all magic . . . ," I say.

"You can't believe in everything," A says, deadpan. Then he turns around and shuffles down the hallway in his wide-wale corduroy pants, *swoosh swoosh swoosh.*

Despite a small headache, I laugh, and way down the stairway I can hear him laughing too.

Pruning

After a biblical period of rain, A and I are in the garden; I see that the rose tree really must be pruned right that second or else it will be too late, winter will be over. I prune carefully with my old dull shears. Nothing more dangerous than a dull tool, I tell A. We work well and quietly side by side for hours. There is no wind. And the roots of weeds and dead plants pull easily now. Sometimes if we pull the opposite way, that also works.

A starts a worm farm. Every time I uproot a weed tree, I yell for A to come see the fresh bugs, the worms oozing out and trying to escape A, who has a handy little spade and a mayonnaise jar.

"They don't know yet that you aren't going to hurt them," I say to A.

Then I find a truly spectacular worm, almost a snake.

"Thank you for finding that big worm, Mommy," A says.

"I'm good at finding worms," I say.

A new neighbor walks by with his wife.

"You going to take out that Scotch broom tree?" he asks.

"What?" I wipe my dirty face. "Oh, that. No, it's too big; no way I can take it."

He steps forward, just like in the movies, and pulls it out, over introductions.

I ask, "Your house built—in what—sixty-five?"

"Sixty-four," they say, grinning. They are now family. They are now tribe members, with the helping, dirty hands to prove it.

"Mine's sixty-five. Any kids?" I ask.

"Nope."

"What's with the dog?" the wife asks.

"Oh, the barking dog in the canyon? Yeah. You won't hear that after a while. The first year it drives you insane. Then you won't even hear it."

In fact, I feel affection toward the dog now, just like the alarm bells that ring every day at twelve noon and five p.m. from the fire station and the frequent and long power outages and the huge rogue tree branches that block the road in storm time, and the red flag fire dangers and everything. It's all become safe house, and the barking dog doesn't signify any longer.

"You can't find that dog," I say to the wife. "I tried, that first year. And I talked to the neighbors in the canyon and I drove around. I think it's this one crazy guy way up Madrone . . . keeps the dog tied up. He should be pretty old by now, that dog. I've been here ten years."

The wife looks unconvinced.

"I swear you will get used to it. Drove me crazy at first. Insane," I say, pulling up a small dead rosemary bush. "Now I don't even hear it."

That's not strictly true. I hear it, but it is a distant sound to me now, one I completely accept. That dog will bark.

The neighbors thank me and I thank them and they leave. A helps me finish the yard job. I am bare-handed and don't want to stop to get my gardening gloves. I am the kind of woman who almost never has a manicure. And my feet are in the earth now too; I can grip the ground better with my bare toes and feet. I am bracing myself using my full weight, to yank up the larger, more entrenched roots. A scrambles for the worms and roly-poly bugs.

This probably started as one rosemary bush and now it's ten big ones, half of them dead wood and choking everything else out, I reflect. And the Scotch broom is of course the garden equivalent of some jeopardous Ubangi virus; you can't kill it entirely ever, you just work around it and manage it. Like time, like loss. Like everything.

I find an old Gatorade bottle and a Saint Christopher medal I buried because Lisa said it would protect my house. I put the medal in my breast pocket. I can actually smell the Friday nightness in the air.

I would like to be the couple with matching Scottish hats returning home up the hill from their daily walk. I'd like to be the doctor across the street and his wife, with their two kids, people who can afford a maid and a babysitter every week; a couple who have each other and haven't been wrecked or cracked open. I would like to have what they share, but it is all right, I know it is out there, know it exists again, love. I don't know how I know; I only know that it's true. I can now think with ease of the travels N and I enjoyed: I can think of the Wine Country again, that too may now exist without pain, the shadows lifting.

In my garden, two huge lavender bushes remain, and the original stones and irrigation system are exposed now. Fresh dirt will be needed. I grab the giant garden shears; I cut everything back, all the jasmine and the camellias and the rose tree.

"You always think it's too much, the pruning, and it never is," I explain to A. "Actually, you can't cut too much or too deep, to save the plant and its roots."

I am wearing red plaid flannel pajamas bottoms, and an inside-out pink Polartec top and my crooked Spencer Tracy glasses. My slipper socks were abandoned by the curb when they got in the way. Yet I feel pretty and capable, almost dazzling.

Somehow I have learned just the rudimentary tips of gardening. There is so much more to learn and think about that it seems all wide and splayed now, but in a good, relaxed way. I am just starting to know things.

"My, my. Look at our yard," I say to A.

A looks on with approval and a red Tootsie Pop sticking from the corner of his mouth like a cigar.

"Now let the worms out, my baby," I say to A. "Even worms have a home."

A bends down wicked low and watches the worms for a long time after he has put them back in the earth.

"Home," he says.

Comet Hale-Bopp

On Saturday mornings in the seventies, we would go grocery shopping, my stepfather and I. He loved to buy meat. We would go to Albertson's and buy a pork loin roast and rye bread and orange juice. Ron has to drag me around the store because I am hugging him and won't let go.

We were at Albertson's Bonanza store when his car was stolen as we were inside, shopping. A yellow Cutlass Supreme, '67. We walked up and down the parking lot aisles, stunned.

He got it back, unharmed. This is Ron's luck. The losing, and the getting back. He once left his wallet on a park bench and the next day it emerged on their front porch in Hayward. It arrived Federal Express, with all the cash intact.

I know instinctively that if my car was ever stolen, I would not get it back. But I also know my car will never be stolen. Just like I knew I would never be a single mother.

One morning N brings coffee as he picks up A. This was always the marriage Saturday morning ritual. Mine with milk, his black. We smile at each other gently, oh so very gently. What hits me is that I finally feel good about being unmarried. But maybe this is not a feeling that is based on being married or unmarried.

It could be that this is the feeling of happiness.

A's father had him for the day while I wrote some copy. Afterward he dropped him off at Bunny's, sleeping. Then, because this is the last possible day, N and I walk far up the nearby King

Acknowledgments

Everything begins and ends with my protean agent, K____
spoon, at Inkwell Management, and her cohort Sally____
CAA, both of whom always make sure the material f____
If every writer writes for three people, I'd cite Haven____
Weldon, and Bunny Mathews. I cannot sufficiently s____
ation to Trena Keating, my wondrous and astut____
championed my life and this book. I honor my exc____
entertaining himself while his mother huddled ir____
what must have seemed like forever to an eight-yea____
ing life is enriched and made feasible by Jon Engd____
man on earth, the Marin County Public School____
Corde Madera Recreation Center. Thanks to L____
Levine, David Forrer, Eric Rindal, Miles Winst____
Housden, Rachelle Marmour, Nick Fox, Lisa S____
McMahon, Holly Virginia Williamson, Ken____
Finnamore, Sabrina Bourg, Chris Lisick, Ly____
Gardner, Seymour Radin, and the extreme and____
Annie Lamott, one Sunday morning when I w____
the third time. Great gratitude to my stepfat____
and to Jason Murray, my loan broker at Ca____
helped save the farm.

KIM EDWARDS

THE MEMORY KEEPER'S DAUGHTER

'Crafted with language so lovely you have to reread the passages just to be captivated all over again' Jodi Picoult

It should have been an ordinary birth, the start of an ordinary happy family. But the night Dr David Henry delivers his wife's twins is a night that will haunt five lives for ever.

For though David's son is a healthy boy, his daughter has Down's syndrome. And, in a shocking act of betrayal whose consequences only time will reveal, he tells his wife their daughter died while secretly entrusting her care to a nurse.

As grief quietly tears apart David's family, so a little girl must make her own way in the world as best she can.

'*The Memory Keeper's Daughter* is an enthralling novel about the deepest secrets that can never stay hidden' *Easy Living*

'Deeply moving. Kim Edward's intricate descriptions and beautiful use of language make this a mesmerising read' *Woman*

'An enthralling tale that will keep you page-turning until well past bedtime. A truly riveting read' *She*

JUDITH O'REILLY

WIFE IN THE NORTH

350 miles from home, three young children and one very absent husband ...

Maybe hormones ate her brain. How else did Judith's husband persuade her to give up her career and move from her beloved London to Northumberland with two toddlers in tow?

Pregnant with number three, Judith is about to discover that there are one or two things about life in the country that no one told her about: that she'd be making friends with people who believe in the four horsemen of the apocalypse; that running out of petrol could be a near-death experience; and that the closest thing to an ethnic minority would be a redhead.

Judith tries to do that simple thing that women do, make hers a happy family. A family that might live happily ever after. Possibly even up North ...

'Funny, poignant and beautifully written' Lisa Jewell

'I howled with laughter, tears of recognition at every page' Jenny Colgan

'Genuinely funny and genuinely moving' Jane Fallon

MARY POLS

ACCIDENTALLY ON PURPOSE

A one-night stand, my unexpected pregnancy, and loving the best mistake I ever made . . .

Mary Pols had always wanted children, but Mr. Right had never come along. Then one night she met a guy. Cute. Much younger. *Definitely* unsuitable. But she went home with him anyway. What was the worst that could happen?

Well, nine months later she was going to find out . . .

As time unfolds, Mary's problems seem to grow as rapidly as her bump. Money. Childcare. How to tell her large, respectable family (especially her dad). Above all, what is she to do about the baby's father? He's sexy but hopeless – almost as much of a boy as her baby-to-be.

Accidentally on Purpose is a funny, heartwarming true story about becoming a mother, finding happiness in the unexpected and compromising in the name of love.

He just wanted a decent book to read ...

Not too much to ask, is it? It was in 1935 when Allen Lane, Managing Director of Bodley Head Publishers, stood on a platform at Exeter railway station looking for something good to read on his journey back to London. His choice was limited to popular magazines and poor-quality paperbacks – the same choice faced every day by the vast majority of readers, few of whom could afford hardbacks. Lane's disappointment and subsequent anger at the range of books generally available led him to found a company – and change the world.

'We believed in the existence in this country of a vast reading public for intelligent books at a low price, and staked everything on it'
Sir Allen Lane, 1902–1970, founder of Penguin Books

The quality paperback had arrived – and not just in bookshops. Lane was adamant that his Penguins should appear in chain stores and tobacconists, and should cost no more than a packet of cigarettes.

Reading habits (and cigarette prices) have changed since 1935, but Penguin still believes in publishing the best books for everybody to enjoy. We still believe that good design costs no more than bad design, and we still believe that quality books published passionately and responsibly make the world a better place.

So wherever you see the little bird – whether it's on a piece of prize-winning literary fiction or a celebrity autobiography, political tour de force or historical masterpiece, a serial-killer thriller, reference book, world classic or a piece of pure escapism – you can bet that it represents the very best that the genre has to offer.

Whatever you like to read – trust Penguin.

Mountain to find the Hale-Bopp comet, twisting higher than we ever have. The trees were obscuring that part of the sky.

I found it first. Then we both found it.

This reminds me of how we fell in love. I saw him and decided. He says he was just admiring my legs, but eventually he decided too. We had a long, ambrosial courtship, the kind that happens to the fortunate. A small wedding, a healthy baby boy.

The comet only appears every seventy-eight years. So you have to get up that hill.

Because you have to see the comet, and because it is rare and precious, even if it ends.